Corporate Entrepreneurship

Entrepreneurship is vital for companies' success, allowing them to adapt and grow in today's interlinked and turbulent business environments. Yet, as they grow in size and complexity, many companies become less innovative, more rigid and risk-averse. The challenge of how to deal with these trends has led to the rise of the field of Corporate Entrepreneurship, looking at the development of new business ideas and opportunities within established firms. This book provides an effective entry point to Corporate Entrepreneurship as an academic field and a management practice.

Corporate Entrepreneurship leads readers through an overview of real-life Corporate Entrepreneurship; the aims, organisational models, implementation process and results. Covering theoretical perspectives, empirical findings and practical concerns, the book also switches between the perspective of the individual and the organisation.

Written by two specialists of the discipline, the book includes a wealth of real-life case studies, covering over three decades of Corporate Entrepreneurship practices, by companies of all sizes, geographies and sectors. With coverage of such topics as Internal Corporate Venturing and Participative Innovation, this thoughtful text will be required reading for entrepreneurship students around the world.

Véronique Bouchard is Professor of Strategy and Organisation. She joined emlyon business school in 2000 after a previous career in strategy consulting. Her research focuses on Corporate Entrepreneurship. She has published numerous articles in international and French-speaking journals. Her last book, *Intrapreneuriat, Innovation et Croissance: Entreprendre dans l'Entreprise*, won the 2010 "Prix du Livre d'Entrepreneuriat".

Alain Fayolle is Professor of Entrepreneurship and Director of the Entrepreneurship Research Centre at emlyon business school. He has published 35 books and over 150 articles in leading journals. He chaired the Academy of Management Entrepreneurship Division in 2016–2017 and acts as an expert for governments and international institutions. He was granted the 2013 European Entrepreneurship Education Award.

"Professors Bouchard and Fayolle have written an insightful, well researched, and practical book. Their valuable contribution to the literature will be welcomed by several audiences, including students, researchers, and managers who seek to learn about the dynamics of Corporate Entrepreneurship."

Jeffrey G. Covin, *Dr., Samuel and Pauline Glaubinger*
Professor of Entrepreneurship, Indiana University

"Corporate Entrepreneurship is essential for today's firms. In this rigorous yet practical book, the authors offer a comprehensive account of the intellectual roots of Corporate Entrepreneurship as a concept, and of the most effective tools to implement it as a practice."

Carlo Salvato, *Bocconi University*

Corporate Entrepreneurship

VÉRONIQUE BOUCHARD AND ALAIN FAYOLLE

Routledge
Taylor & Francis Group

LONDON AND NEW YORK

First published 2018
by Routledge
2 Park Square, Milton Park, Abingdon, Oxon OX14 4RN

and by Routledge
711 Third Avenue, New York, NY 10017

Routledge is an imprint of the Taylor & Francis Group, an informa business

© 2018 Véronique Bouchard and Alain Fayolle

British Library Cataloguing-in-Publication Data
A catalogue record for this book is available from the British Library

Library of Congress Cataloging-in-Publication Data
Names: Bouchard, Véronique, 1958- author. | Fayolle, Alain, author.
Title: Corporate entrepreneurship/Véronique Bouchard and Alain Fayolle.
Description: 1 Edition. | New York: Routledge, 2018. |
Includes bibliographical references.
Identifiers: LCCN 2017032504 | ISBN 9781138813670 | ISBN 9781138813687 |
ISBN 9781315747989 (eISBN)
Subjects: LCSH: Entrepreneurship. | Teams in the workplace–Management. |
Organizational change.
Classification: LCC HB615.B6687 2018 | DDC 658.4/21–dc23
LC record available at https://lccn.loc.gov/2017032504

ISBN: 978-1-138-81367-0 (hbk)
ISBN: 978-1-138-81368-7 (pbk)
ISBN: 978-1-315-74798-9 (ebk)

Typeset in Dante
by Sunrise Setting Ltd, Brixham, UK

Dedication

In memory of Nicola del Forno

Contents

Figures

Tables

Introduction

The learning journey

Entrepreneurship, defined in Wikipedia as "the capacity and willingness to develop, organize and manage a business venture along with any of its risks in order to make a profit", is at the origin of all successful companies. But as they grow in size and complexity, companies become increasingly dependent on dominant market positions and fine-tuned internal processes for their success. They become less innovative, more rigid and risk-adverse: in one word, less entrepreneurial. Yet in increasingly turbulent and global environments, established firms cannot survive unless they are ready to put their gains back into play to conquer new markets, harness new technologies and invent new business models. All these challenges require Entrepreneurship... Corporate Entrepreneurship to be precise...

Nevertheless, many scholars view Corporate Entrepreneurship as being a contradiction in terms. Stevenson and Gumpert (1985) underline the limits that "high level decisions and the exigencies of the hierarchy" impose on entrepreneurial behaviours and Kanter et al. (1990, 1991a, 1991b) depict the problematic coexistence of the "newstream" (the flow of intra-entrepreneurial initiatives) with the "mainstream" in any given company. Stevenson and Jarillo (1990) and Thornberry (2001) even call it an "oxymoron". Yet, over the years, many companies have put in place plans, processes, systems and organisational structures whose ultimate goal is to foster Corporate Entrepreneurship, some with mixed results, but others with considerable success, indicating that Corporate Entrepreneurship is elusive but not beyond reach.

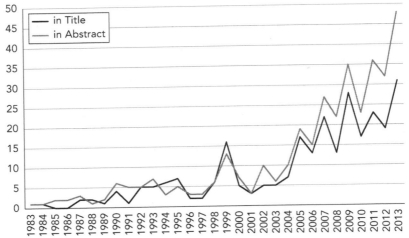

Figure I.1 An increasingly popular topic

Source: Proquest – Scholarly journals (1983–2013).

In spite of its inner contradictions, or maybe because of them, Corporate Entrepreneurship is a fascinating object of study and one that has gained considerable momentum in the last decade (see Figure I.1).

Corporate Entrepreneurship is not only contradictory, it is also a multi-faceted concept that means different things to different people: some scholars and most practitioners view it as an **intra-firm process** leading to new business development, while others, mostly academics, view it as a **firm-level strategic posture** that is geared towards innovation, proactiveness and risk-taking. Additional ambiguities arise from the fact that two terms – Intrapreneurship and Corporate Venturing – are used in the literature as quasi-synonyms of Corporate Entrepreneurship.

Corporate Entrepreneurship being a complex and ambiguous concept, the reader's learning path should start with a broad overview of its various connotations both in the business world and in academia. The first part of this book, "Exploring Corporate Entrepreneurship" outlines the **reality** of Corporate Entrepreneurship: why companies try to encourage it, how they implement it, what benefits can be obtained in practice and so on. It then summarises **academic production** on Corporate Entrepreneurship, with a brief review of the literature and an examination of its **definitions and definitional issues.** Finally, the notion of **entrepreneurial orientation** is explored thanks to an in-depth case study.

Corporate Entrepreneurship is viewed by the layman as "entrepreneurship within the corporation": is this simple view acceptable? To answer this question, one needs to observe carefully how the Corporate Entrepreneurship process unfolds in practice, using Independent Entrepreneurship as a benchmark and comparing them. In the second part of this book, "Understanding the Corporate Entrepreneurship process", the reader will discover the different facets of the **Corporate Entrepreneurship process**. Various models suggested in the literature will be reviewed and an original model will be presented. We will then look at **team interaction and management** in a Corporate Entrepreneurship context.

In the third part of this book, "Implementing Corporate Entrepreneurship: learning from experience", we will review **what companies do in order to foster Corporate Entrepreneurship**. We will delve deep into their actual practices, exploiting a set of first-hand and second-hand case studies covering several countries and decades. More specifically, we will review and assess **the managerial and organisational tools** most commonly used to foster Corporate Entrepreneurship, then look at how companies **combine those tools into ad hoc organisational devices** to instil entrepreneurial values and behaviours among employees, create environments that are favourable to innovation and risk-taking, and for a few of them, durably combine large size and Entrepreneurial Orientation. To conclude this part, we will present **the basic design principles** that underlie all Corporate Entrepreneurship implementation attempts, emphasising their dynamics and impact on individuals and organisations.

Methodology and sources

Throughout this book, we will be presenting conceptual models and making assertions that reflect state-of-the-art research in the field of Corporate Entrepreneurship, as well as originating from our own observation and analysis of actual practices. In order to cast a wide net on Corporate Entrepreneurship practices, we have collected and analysed a broad and diverse set of case studies. Over time, we have gathered a total of 30 cases providing detailed descriptions of Corporate Entrepreneurship practices in a variety of well-established firms (cf. Appendix 1). Our database contains seven first-hand cases and 23 second-hand cases.

The seven first-hand cases included in the study were created and published over a ten-year period (2003 to 2012) by the authors. They provide detailed descriptions of Corporate Entrepreneurship practices implemented in medium to large-size European firms representing various industries.

The 23 second-hand cases included in our case base originate from material drawn from reputable sources such as top ranking academic journals, highly regarded professional publications or the case clearinghouses of top educational institutions. Second-hand sources were searched for in electronic databases using the following keywords: *corporate entrepreneur**, *intrapreneur** and *corporate ventur**.

In summary

☐ Since its emergence in the early 1980s, the topic of Corporate Entrepreneurship has gained prominence in both business and academia. Yet, Corporate Entrepreneurship remains an elusive notion, contradictory in terms, meaning different things to different people.

☐ This book aims at providing an effective entry point into Corporate Entrepreneurship, envisioned both as a set of managerial practices and a research field.

☐ A three-leg path is proposed to the learner: in Part 1, the notion of Corporate Entrepreneurship is explored and defined; in Part 2, the process of Corporate entrepreneurship is scrutinised; and in Part 3, the forms that Corporate Entrepreneurship take in practice and the challenges its implementation raises are presented and discussed.

☐ Most of the observations and statements contained in this book result from the analysis by the authors of a large body of first-hand and second-hand case studies (cf. Appendix 1).

Part 1

Exploring Corporate Entrepreneurship

Corporate Entrepreneurship being a complex and ambiguous concept, our learning journey starts with the exploration of the various forms it takes in business organisations and in the literature. This first part includes:

- An overview of the practice of Corporate Entrepreneurship over a three-decade period: why companies encourage it, how they implement it, what benefits are obtained and what issues are raised (Chapter 1).
- A summary of the research on Corporate Entrepreneurship from the 1980s on, emphasising its definitional issues (Chapter 2).
- An in-depth case study, "Corporate Entrepreneurship at L'Oréal", that will allow the reader to integrate practice and theory (Chapter 3).

Corporate Entrepreneurship in Practice: an overview

1

The concept of corporate entrepreneurship has been around for at least 20 years. Broadly speaking, it refers to the development of new business ideas and opportunities within large and established corporations.

(Birkinshaw, 2003)[1]

First, though, what exactly is Corporate Entrepreneurship? We define the term as the process by which teams within an established company conceive, foster, launch and manage a new business that is distinct from the parent company but leverages the parent's assets, market position, capabilities or other resources.

(Wolcott and Lippitz, 2007a)[2]

Introduction

As these definitions suggest, Corporate Entrepreneurship refers to the **development of new businesses within established firms**. It involves internal teams and leverages internal resources. We will see later that Corporate Entrepreneurship is indeed broader and more complex but this first definition is sufficient to initiate our exploration. In this overview, we will see that Corporate Entrepreneurship can be either a **spontaneous** or **management-induced** process (see Figure 1.1). We will then describe its **benefits**, explore its relation to **innovation** and, finally, review some recurrent **issues** tied to its implementation.

Spontaneous Corporate Entrepreneurship	*Induced Corporate Entrepreneurship*
An unplanned process triggered by employees who engage spontaneously in the development of a new activity within an established firm using the "slack resources" of the company.	The managerial practices that companies adopt in order to encourage and support the development of new activities by employees and the outcome of these practices.

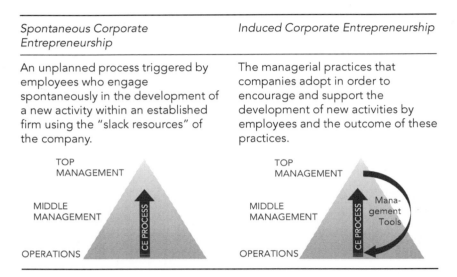

Figure 1.1 Spontaneous versus Induced Corporate Entrepreneurship

The forthcoming chapters will refer to several of these cases contained in our extensive database (cf. Appendix 1).

Corporate Entrepreneurship as a spontaneous process

Well-established companies periodically benefit from the determination and talent of managers or employees who identify and seize business opportunities that were not envisioned by the top management team. According to Burgelman (1983MS), this phenomenon is inherent in the nature of large organisations. Large organisations have "organisational slack"; that is:

> [A] cushion of actual or potential resources which allow them to adapt successfully to internal pressures for adjustment or to external pressures for change in policy, as well as to initiate changes in strategy with respect to the external environment.
>
> (Cyert and March, 1963, p. 36)

Employees who have ideas can access these slack resources to explore and develop their project and some of them manage to do so successfully.

In a large firm, at any given point in time, there are normally several employees eager to pursue an initiative. As long as they have access to the resources they need, a number of them will manage to bring their project to completion, thus enlarging the scope of activities of the firm (Burgelman, 1983MS). We call this phenomenon "Spontaneous Corporate Entrepreneurship". Spontaneous Corporate Entrepreneurship can be seen as a **bottom-up process** that complements the top-down strategic planning process and thus contributes to the strategic renewal of the firm.

Just as autonomous initiatives "spontaneously" emerge, the existing organisation – the "mainstream" to use Kanter and North's terminology (1990) – "spontaneously" resists these initiatives and sometimes crushes them. This "mainstream" / "newstream" opposition has been described and analysed in a number of articles and business cases (cf. Burgelman, 1983MS; Hill, Kamprath and Conrad, 1992; Dougherty and Hardy, 1996; Hamel, 2000). The profound differences that characterise the part of the organisation that is involved in reproducing, administrating, optimising and controlling – the "mainstream" – to the part of the organisation that is involved in experimenting and creating – the "newstream" – leads to tensions, misunderstandings and even conflicts. Focus on short versus long-term results, attitude towards risk and acceptance of errors, respect of rules and procedures and reliance on informal networks are all dimensions on which the "mainstream" and the "newstream" radically diverge. The frictions these differences generate, amplified by turf wars, can lead to open or masked conflicts, which often end to the detriment of the weaker "newstream".

What inspires "spontaneous" corporate entrepreneurs? They are, for the most part, guided by intrinsic motivations. Indeed, Corporate Entrepreneurship requires such efforts and involves such potential frustrations, that calculation is rarely the trigger. Two recurrent motivations stand out: first, corporate entrepreneurs believe that they act for the good of the company and that without their project the company would miss an opportunity; second, they are in search of greater autonomy, job satisfaction, self-affirmation and personal recognition. Clearly, these two motivations often coexist.

The motivations of corporate entrepreneurs are mostly intrinsic but this does not imply that they do not expect something in return: perhaps they want to manage the activity they have created, be promoted, get recognition, a bonus, a salary increase or a sabbatical. Initially, this remains a matter of conjecture, as corporate entrepreneurs seldom have clear expectations and almost never spell them out loud when they engage in a project.

Box 1.1 The MEMS Unit: a case of Spontaneous Corporate Entrepreneurship

The MEMS Unit (MMU) is an autonomous "entrepreneurial entity" created in January 2004 within the SBL group[3] at the initiative of Eric D. Eric D. had the idea to commercially exploit the MEMS technology[4] while he was Head of Research at a laboratory located in New England. He was turning 40 and looking for a new challenge. During his numerous discussions with senior management, Eric D. requested to have "carte blanche" as to the location of the activity and the choice of employees. He believed that his success strongly depended on the quality of engineers, technical partners and subcontractors with whom he would collaborate and he chose to return to France and reconnect with his former acquaintances. Thus was created the MMU, a new profit centre whose purpose was to develop and commercialise innovative technologies developed in the labs of the group: from its inception, it had the full support of the senior management of SBL keen to encourage innovation and promote entrepreneurial values.

Eric D. came back to France and found a site in the Paris suburbs and immediately put a clean room under construction. The material required for the manufacturing and testing of prototypes was purchased second-hand or recovered in other labs of the group. Eric D. surrounded himself with technically qualified and resourceful people able to face the many challenges and practical difficulties typical of the start-up phase of a business. He made sure everyone felt accountable by setting clear goals and reviewing them with his team regularly. Relationship management with the parent company was taken very seriously. The MMU, a tiny entity in terms of the SBL group, had to gain visibility while preserving its room for manoeuvre: targeted communication and internal networking were therefore strategic activities. Twenty-four months after its creation, the results of the MMU were very positive. Internal customers had approved two products and word of mouth began to take effect, opening new business prospects. The development speed of the MMU and the technical performance of its products, in spite of the entity's limited means, surprised many inside SBL.

Source: Adapted from Bouchard (2009E).

As can be seen in this example, "spontaneous" corporate entrepreneurs can bring very tangible benefits to companies. If Corporate Entrepreneurship does contribute to growth and innovation, to strategic renewal even, should it not it be deliberately encouraged? Many companies answer this question with a yes and attempt to put in place tools and processes that aim at **inducing** Corporate Entrepreneurship.

Induced Corporate Entrepreneurship

Unlike spontaneous Corporate Entrepreneurship, **induced** Corporate Entrepreneurship is triggered by a combination of management actions and tools such as top management communication, ad hoc incentives and rewards, training programmes, project selection procedures and so on. Some employees, who might otherwise not have taken the plunge, will respond favourably to these actions and tools and decide to push forward – with the approval and support of the organisation – their own "entrepreneurial" project.

Over the last three decades, well-known companies such as the Xerox Corporation, Lucent Technologies, 3M or Gore in the United States and Schneider Electric, Siemens Nixdorf and Nestlé in Europe have devised and implemented their own combination of tools and actions to foster entrepreneurial initiatives. Several articles and case studies[5] describe in detail what we will call "Corporate Entrepreneurship Devices" from now on; that is, an ad hoc combination of managerial and organisational tools designed and implemented by the management of established companies in order to induce Corporate Entrepreneurship.

Box 1.2 The Stockeasy project: a case of Induced Corporate Entrepreneurship

We are at the turn of the century and the French company Schneider Electric has reached a global leadership position in electrical equipment and industrial automation thanks to an ambitious strategy of mergers and acquisitions. These mergers and acquisitions, however, have dampened the internal growth dynamic of the company. Elaborated by the head of Strategy France, "A Myriad of Ideas" is a programme that aims at "revitalizing" the French business unit. At meetings held across the territory, the head of strategy preaches the good word to hundreds of managers, urging them to innovate and take initiatives. He promises that proposals, wherever they originated, will be evaluated and that the best will receive funding and support from a team of experts.

Jean-Marc R., a local manager, learned about "A Myriad of Ideas" during a presentation by a Strategy Department "evangelist". He whole-heartedly embraced the philosophy of the programme, which corresponded to his personal vision of business and management: "From the beginning, I was interested in the process... And I immediately inserted four or five ideas in the database". Among them, was the idea to create a business to manage local stocks of high turnover spare parts to better serve Schneider Electric's clients. Jean-Marc's idea was one of the first to be reviewed by the officials of "A Myriad of Ideas". After discussing it with him, they encouraged Jean-Marc to refine his project and assess its feasibility. Jean-Marc was granted one day per week to work on the project and a budget of €24,000 to perform market research. The research produced encouraging results and the project was vetted for the next stage. But the important working capital requirements of the project scared Jean-Marc. Fortunately, a few months later, an enthusiastic colleague decided to join him, giving Jean-Marc extra confidence in his project. The project was approved by the Executive Committee of Schneider Electric who granted the two associates a budget of €760,000 and access the company's venture funding scheme. The "Stockeasy" company was created: Schneider Electric owned 80 per cent of the shares and the two associates 10 per cent each. A few months later, the first spare parts were delivered to Schneider Electric's clients. When asked about the whole process, Jean-Marc R. concluded with these words: "I was very lucky to be able to develop my business idea within Schneider Electric. I would not have managed on my own, but in this secure business environment, it's been an amazing experience".

Source: Adapted from Bouchard (2009IIC).

There are many ways to induce Corporate Entrepreneurship. The minimalist approach is characterised by its limited scope and ambition. In this approach, top management creates the conditions that will help the **completion of specific projects**, deemed particularly important or attractive. Senior managers approve or pick the team of corporate entrepreneurs, grant them autonomy and resources and usually place them under their direct supervision. In exchange, corporate entrepreneurs are expected to effectively and rapidly develop, test and commercialise their new business idea.

Other companies opt for a more ambitious approach and put in place Corporate Entrepreneurship Devices whose aim is to encourage a **steady flow of entrepreneurial initiatives**. The management and organisational tools implemented include incentive systems, training programmes, project evaluation procedures, dedicated organisational entities and so on. When appropriately designed and managed, Corporate Entrepreneurship Devices can have a significant impact on the behaviour of employees, encouraging the hatching of hundreds of entrepreneurial projects each year. There are dual benefits of this approach: (1) employees feel more motivated because they know they are allowed to propose and work on a project they really care for (even if they decide not to); (2) new products, new client segments and new internal processes see the light and usually get developed much faster than via conventional routes.

Finally, some companies require **all their staff to embrace entrepreneurial values and behave entrepreneurially**. They usually are innovative, fast growing firms with atypical culture, organisation and management styles. There are not many companies in which entrepreneurial values and behaviours are mainstream: for decades, 3M has been cited as the example of a large entrepreneurial firm. W.L. Gore and Associates is another less cited but interesting example. Lately, Alphabet (Google) has emerged as the quintessence of the large entrepreneurial company. And as we will see in Chapter 3, L'Oréal also falls into this category.

Corporate Entrepreneurship: motivations and benefits

Corporate Entrepreneurship is currently a hot topic within the business community. Whether the term in use is Corporate Entrepreneurship, Intrapreneurship or Corporate Venturing, there is a wide recognition that established firms imperatively need to maintain and/or promote entrepreneurial values, attitudes and approaches. The concept of Corporate Entrepreneurship began to gain currency in the US in the early 1980s, as a wave of deregulation forced well-established companies from various sectors (transportation, finance, telecom, etc.) to question their strategy and management approaches. To stimulate an internal dynamic of change that would result in improved employee commitment and corporate performance, companies such as Ohio Bell, the New England Electric Systems, Eastman Kodak and SAS, designed and implemented original Corporate Entrepreneurship Devices.

The late 1990s were marked, both in the US and Europe, by the emergence of a pro-entrepreneurial culture and the diffusion of entrepreneurs and start-ups as success models. As the first Internet Revolution unfolded, established firms became acutely aware of the growing importance of innovation and embraced Corporate Entrepreneurship as a means to improve their performance by better leveraging intangible assets – proprietary technologies, unique competencies, brands – but also to retain talented employees otherwise tempted to leave the company to create their own business. Among these companies, we can cite Procter & Gamble, Nokia, Siemens Nixdorf, Schneider Electric and Lucent Technologies.

In the past decade, the interest for Corporate Entrepreneurship has increased considerably:[6] companies from all sectors are now facing technological disruptions and fierce global competition and there is a wide recognition that innovation is an absolute imperative. Furthermore, Corporate Entrepreneurship appears particularly well-suited to a new generation of employees that value creativity, task variety and autonomy in the workplace and dream of creating their own business at some point in their life.

As Kanter et al. already noted in a 1990 article, the rationale for inducing Corporate Entrepreneurship is two-fold: companies pursue both "economic goals" (increased revenues, innovation, return on assets, etc.) and "cultural goals" (happier, more productive, more engaged employees). This remains true to this day and many of the strongest promoters of Corporate Entrepreneurship can be found in Human Resources Management departments.

Corporate Entrepreneurship is also viewed as a cure to some organisational dysfunctions and ailments. Examining our case database, we identified five recurrent issues at the origin of the decision to encourage Corporate Entrepreneurship (see Box 1.3).

Box 1.3 Why do companies decide to foster Corporate Entrepreneurship?

(1) To revitalise the organisation

Because they have gone through a series of mergers and acquisitions or because of poor management, some companies seem to lose a sense of purpose and see the level of engagement of employees decline drastically. In this context, the promotion of entrepreneurial values, attitudes and processes is seen by the top management as a way to re-engage disheartened employees and improve the corporate climate, as well as opening new vistas and providing space for creativity and autonomy.

(2) To increase speed and responsiveness

Organisations that are large and complex are usually slow and rigid in their decision and implementation processes. They cannot adapt to fast-changing market needs or readily respond to new competitive challenges. In this case, the adoption of entrepreneurial values, attitudes and processes is viewed first and foremost as a means to increase responsiveness and reduce time-to-market.

(3) To better capitalise on intangible assets

Many companies invest heavily in R&D but do not fully exploit the intangible assets (inventions, patents, know-how, etc.) they generate. In this case, the adoption of entrepreneurial values, attitudes and processes is seen as a tool that can help extract more value from these assets.

(4) To grow abroad

In some sectors (retail, food and beverages, personal care, for example), foreign market entries require deep local adaptation of the product, marketing mix and management style. In this case, the adoption of entrepreneurial values, attitudes and processes allows country managers to autonomously explore local conditions, adapt strategies and create viable organisations, with minimum interference from headquarters.

But what are the actual benefits of encouraging Corporate Entrepreneurship? Our analysis shows that there are four categories of benefits (see Figure 1.2).

Economic performance

Companies that implement Corporate Entrepreneurship in earnest witness a blossom of new projects that leverage existing resources and help generate new revenue streams (see Table 1.1).

Generally speaking, the development cost of entrepreneurial projects is low because it relies in good part on "slack resources" and, consequently, return on investment is high. However, because the revenues generated thanks to Corporate Entrepreneurship usually represent only a small percentage of the total turnover of the company, managers who, rightly or wrongly, have high revenue expectations when they put in place Corporate Entrepreneurship initiatives can feel disappointed.

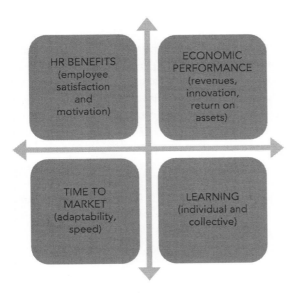

Figure 1.2 The benefits of Corporate Entrepreneurship

Table 1.1 Some economic benefits of Corporate Entrepreneurship

Case study	Economic results
Raytheon	Over 20 years, 50 new products generating several hundred M$ revenues per year.
Eastman Kodak	Over five years, 14 new internal ventures marginally contributing to the company's total turnover.
Ohio Bell	Over five years, 500 projects contributing 14 M$.
Xerox Corporation	Over five years, 12 new businesses with high return on investment but marginally contributing to the company's total turnover.
Lucent Technologies	After five years, a portfolio of 26 new businesses, 200 M$ incremental value, internal rate of return > 70 per cent. One several hundred M$ initial public offering (IPO). Marginal contribution to the company's total turnover.

Source: cf. Appendix 1.

Improved employee motivation and corporate climate

On this front too, Corporate Entrepreneurship can work remarkably well. Well-conceived Corporate Entrepreneurship Devices elicit a great deal of enthusiasm and involvement on the part of employees. In large organisations, it is not rare to witness the participation of several hundred employees. Participants report that the early implementation phases are coloured with strong positive feelings. They also declare that their involvement in developing a project led them to contact many different people outside their department and, overall, led to improved horizontal and vertical communication, as well as increased cooperation. In some cases, however, corporate entrepreneurs can be extremely negative about their experience: this happens when their expectations in terms of support, guidance and rewards have not been met by the organisation. They can feel cheated and some of them can even decide to leave the company.

Speed and responsiveness

A very important benefit of Corporate Entrepreneurship is the acceleration of development cycles and the reduction of time-to-market. This results from one of Corporate Entrepreneurship's defining features, namely, the importance given to individuals *qua* individuals at all development stages. Individuals, not organisations, detect opportunities and trigger learning processes. Only individuals can couple in their mind all the dimensions – technologies, resources, market requirements – of business development, respond quickly to new information and instantaneously modify their course of action. As a consequence, corporate entrepreneurs move and adapt faster than their bureaucratic and process-constrained counterparts. Paradoxically, they are also less constrained by time, not being expected to produce economic results in the short-term. The different "clock" of corporate entrepreneurs is a two-edged sword: it can accelerate the pulse of the whole organisation or, on the contrary, generate considerable internal tension.

Individual and organisational learning

Because it modifies organisational routines, Corporate Entrepreneurship triggers learning processes both at the individual and collective level. New skills are acquired and additional knowledge is developed about new markets and technologies. Corporate entrepreneurs acquire new management skills, learn about business development and how to interact with the various departments and stakeholders of the company. In the process of completing their project, they become politically savvy, well-connected generalists. Organisations, for their part, progressively learn to leave space for non-conformist ideas and behaviours and to support the individuals that embody them. Such important benefits are unfortunately difficult to measure with standard performance measurement tools and are rarely taken into consideration when performing a cost/benefit analysis of Corporate Entrepreneurship.

Corporate Entrepreneurship and innovation

> Today's businesses, especially the large ones, simply will not survive in this period of rapid change and innovation unless they acquire entrepreneurial competence.
>
> (Peter F. Drucker)

> [T]he notion of innovation is at the very core of corporate entrepreneurship – the two inseparably bound together and responsible for driving calculated and beneficial risk-taking.
>
> (Ryan May)[7]

> Cost-effective innovation happens when someone becomes the passionate champion of a new idea and acts with great courage to push it through the system despite the "Not Invented Here" syndrome, and all the other forms of resistance which large organizations supply.
>
> (Pinchot, 1987)[8]

As these quotes suggest, a strong link exists between Corporate Entrepreneurship and innovation. The authors suggest that entrepreneurial competence, risk acceptance and committed and persistent champions are critical conditions for more and faster innovation within established firms.

Innovation is the process of converting an idea or invention into a good or service that creates value that users are willing to adopt and/or pay for. This conversion process remains elusive to many well-established companies who spend massive amounts of money on R&D, with little return at the end of the line. Companies from various sectors and geographies are presently quite dissatisfied with their innovation capability, which they deem slow, poorly integrated and based on insufficient knowledge of the customer (Boston Consulting Group, 2014). For more and more of them, Corporate Entrepreneurship now stands out as one important element of the solution.

Corporate Entrepreneurship can in fact be viewed as *an approach to innovation that does not rely on institutionalised processes and competencies but leverages individual impetus and improvisation* (Tzeng, 2009).

Table 1.2 Institutionalised Innovation versus Corporate Entrepreneurship

Institutionalised Innovation	Corporate Entrepreneurship
Project is legitimate from the start	Legitimacy of project is established along the way
Funding is guaranteed	Uncertain and conditional funding
Prerogative of certain departments (R&D and marketing usually)	Can originate anywhere in the organisation
Relies on collective effort and is based on established procedures and circuits	Relies on individual initiatives, informal networks and ad hoc procedures (at least initially)
Low personalisation and high specialisation of tasks	High personalisation and low specialisation of tasks
Collective rewards/sanctions	Personal rewards/sanctions

One of the characteristics of this approach is that it puts individuals (or small groups of individuals) and their social interactions at the centre of the innovation process. Corporate entrepreneurs are first and foremost committed, autonomous individuals who behave as partners of the organisation and not as cogs. They do not contribute to the innovation process as specialists but take care of all aspects of their project throughout its various phases. They do not rely on a pre-defined financial envelope but have to "sell" their projects internally in order to get the needed resources. It is also common for corporate entrepreneurs to work on projects on top of their other activities, at least in the initial stages. They rely on informal networks to get resources and support and do not necessary follow standard procedures. Finally, corporate entrepreneurs are willing to take personal responsibility for the success and failure of their project. Thanks to this behaviour, corporate entrepreneurs accelerate development and increase the chances of success of innovative projects. They also take more personal risk than their bureaucratic counterparts (see Table 1.2).

Institutionalised Innovation and Corporate Entrepreneurship are not mutually exclusive processes and can, in fact, coexist and complement each other. One key decision, when fostering Corporate Entrepreneurship, regards its **scope**: what departments and divisions should be encouraged to go beyond Institutionalised Innovation? What employees should be encouraged to become corporate entrepreneurs? What kind of initiatives should be supported? The scope of Corporate Entrepreneurship can be narrow, with a focus on high potential projects, for example, or broad, embracing all kinds of employee initiatives; it can be local – concerning one division only – or global – impacting the whole organisation.

The mixed results of Corporate Entrepreneurship

Corporate Entrepreneurship can be adopted in a variety of contexts to pursue a wide range of corporate objectives, and thus, its appeal to the business world. Empirical evidence shows, however, that Corporate Entrepreneurship is not that easy to implement and companies face recurrent issues when doing so.

Some academics (Stevenson and Jarillo, 1990; Thornberry, 2001) have gone as far as questioning the viability of Corporate Entrepreneurship, which they deem an "oxymoron". They argue that Corporate Entrepreneurship is a destined-to-fail attempt at reconciling incompatible sets of values and approaches: we personally defend a less extreme position, and although aware of the inherent contradictions of Corporate Entrepreneurship, we believe these contradictions can be managed. After all, complex organisations are rife with incompatible processes and conflicting goals and a key task of managers is to transcend or balance these oppositions. The successful implementation of Corporate Entrepreneurship requires leaders and key actors that are fully aware of the tensions that inevitably arise between the "newstream" and the "mainstream" and can find ways to alleviate them.

The academic literature and our case analysis indicate that several issues are associated with the implementation of Corporate Entrepreneurship. The following are among the most common:

- "Newstream"/"mainstream" conflicts;
- outcomes not meeting expectations;
- lack of strategic alignment of some employee initiatives;
- greater risk of losing valuable employees; and
- hard-to-measure benefits sometimes leading to fluctuating commitment on the part of senior managers.

"Newstream"/"mainstream" conflicts

The inherent tensions between the "mainstream" and the "newstream" have been described by various scholars (Fast, 1978; Burgelman and Sayles, 1986; Block and MacMillan, 1993; Kanter et al., 1990; Chesbrough, 2000; Gompers and Lerner, 2000). Tensions, which in theory could be productive, lead, more often than not, to destructive conflicts. Corporate entrepreneurs fight with managers of established operating divisions because of issues that range from disagreements over respective territories, competition over shared resources and culture clashes, to feelings of envy and mistrust. The hierarchy, for its part, does not always apply what it preaches and finds it hard to grant real autonomy to employees. Corporate entrepreneurs can experience conflict with their superiors because they feel misunderstood and poorly supported. Disagreements over performance measurements and adequate rewards are also commonplace.

Outcomes not meeting expectations

In companies that already generate massive revenues, it is rarely possible for individuals to identify and develop comparable opportunities: the revenues generated will at best represent a small percentage of the total company's turnover. Corporate Entrepreneurship's impact is also limited by the organisational and political obstacles employees find on their way. Corporate entrepreneurs have to fight constantly for resources and support and many of them continue to perform their regular job in parallel: in such conditions, only the most talented and motivated ones manage to successfully complete their project. Organisational resistance and political feuds tend to select out all but the most motivated and savvy, ultimately impacting negatively the innovation and revenue generation potential of Corporate Entrepreneurship (Burgelman, 1983MS; Kanter et al., 1991a, 1991b; Hamel, 2000).

Lack of strategic alignment of employee initiatives

It is not possible to rely on personal initiative and commitment without increasing the autonomy of individuals and consequently the risk that their personal projects might diverge from the strategic orientations of the firm. An effective Corporate Entrepreneurship Device normally elicits a large number of initiatives, whose degree of relatedness to the corporation's core activities cannot be fully determined in advance. To this extent, Corporate Entrepreneurship can be seen as diverting valuable resources away from the strategic priorities of the firm: technical and financial resources, of course, but above all, the time and mental energy of highly skilled managers and technologists (Greene, Brush and Hart, 1999). It can also be seen as a practice whose outcomes can potentially blur the company's position and image. We will see later that a well-designed project selection process, able to control divergence without killing creativity, is indeed at the heart of all successful Corporate Entrepreneurship implementation attempts.

Risk of losing valuable employees

When a corporation relies on single individuals to foster innovation rather than on institutional R&D teams and their well-established routines, it indirectly favours the development of highly mobile resources at the expense of more embedded ones. In effect, the key resource of Corporate Entrepreneurship is the corporate entrepreneur himself (Greene, Brush and Hart, 1999), a highly mobile resource. Experienced corporate entrepreneurs possess firm-specific skills – their knowledge and mastery of markets, technologies and internal processes – but also valuable generic skills, which they acquire and reinforce as they go through the various stages of the venture process. These later skills are highly marketable and can facilitate the exit of corporate entrepreneurs. Their departure can imply a significant loss in both human and social capital (Dess and Shaw, 2001).

Hard-to-measure benefits leading to fluctuating commitment of senior managers

Studies have shown that few Corporate Entrepreneurship Devices last for more than a few years (Fast, 1978; Kanter et al., 1990; Block and MacMillan, 1993). Dismantling can be circumstantial (e.g. due to the arrival of a new CEO), dictated by a shift in strategic priorities but, very often, it is a consequence of the inability of Corporate Entrepreneurship promoters to properly measure and internally "sell" its benefits. Benefits such as increased motivation, enhanced creativity or organisational learning are hard to measure and, as a consequence, undervalued. Corporate Entrepreneurship Devices are also criticised because of their lack of synergies with the rest of the organisation. Not surprisingly, they constitute "unstable organizational forms" (Kanter et al., 1990) that are easily disposed of by the next top management team.

In summary

This chapter provides an overview of the reality of Corporate Entrepreneurship, the forms it takes, the rationale behind its adoption, the benefits it brings and the issues it raises.

Key points:

☐ In common parlance, Corporate Entrepreneurship refers to the development of new businesses within established firms.

☐ Corporate Entrepreneurship takes place spontaneously within organisations. Studies show that when they can have access to the slack resources of the organisation, employees engage autonomously in the development of innovative projects.

☐ Corporate Entrepreneurship can also be encouraged thanks to various management and organisational tools. We call the set of tools and actions specifically put together by managers to foster Corporate Entrepreneurship, "Corporate Entrepreneurship Devices".

☐ When implementing Corporate Entrepreneurship, managers pursue both "economic goals" (increased revenues, innovation, return on assets, etc.) and "cultural goals" (happier, more innovative and engaged employees).

☐ The observable benefits of Corporate Entrepreneurship are: (1) improved economic performance; (2) improved climate and employee motivation; (3) shorter development cycles and improved organisational responsiveness; and (4) individual and organisational learning.

☐ Corporate Entrepreneurship is increasingly viewed as inseparable from Innovation. Corporate Entrepreneurship can in fact be seen as an approach to innovation that emphasises the initiative, talent and social skills of individuals. It complements and sustains institutionalised innovation processes.

☐ Empirical evidence shows that Corporate Entrepreneurship is not easy to implement and that it raises recurrent issues such as: (1) "new-stream"/"mainstream" conflicts; (2) outcomes not meeting expectations; (3) lack of strategic alignment of some employee initiatives; (4) greater risk of losing valuable employees; and (5) hard-to-measure benefits sometimes leading to fluctuating commitment on the part of senior managers.

To go further

Read the mini-case in Box 1.4 and answer the questions at the end.

Box 1.4 The TV on ADSL project

The story of Silvia and the TV on ADSL project begins in 2001, a very difficult year for the group in which Silvia works. This large telecommunications company is highly indebted and its traditional markets are rapidly eroding. The board of the "Landline" division, which is particularly affected, is trying to react by encouraging the development of new activities. In April 2001, an incubator is created within the division and Silvia is appointed as manager. She is given the assignment of seeking out some "gems" in the group's labs and accelerating their marketing. In her career of some 15 years, Silvia, a telecom engineer, has acquired a well-rounded profile as well as solid project management experience. Silvia identifies three "gems" at various stages of development and recruits three project managers internally whose mission is to define a viable business model, develop a business plan and test these promising products in real-life conditions. The project managers have to work in pairs with marketing specialists from other divisions but right from the start, the "marketers" contacted seem very reluctant to cooperate. One of the three products selected by Silvia is TV on ADSL.

TV using ADSL makes it possible for users to receive a multi-channel package and to have access to video services on demand (VOD) through their telephone line. The R&D teams are convinced of the product's technical feasibility, but as for the rest, everything still remains very nebulous. Silvia and her project manager have to devise everything, from the network architecture to the business model. The project starts with a budget of €800,000 and it is tackled from a decidedly technical angle. The first stages of the project are writing the technical specifications, working-out the calls for tender and selecting suppliers and technical partners for the pilot project. After a few months, the strategic value of the TV on ADSL project becomes quite clear in the eyes of Silvia and her superiors. The two other projects are abandoned and two additional engineers are allocated to the project.

At the end of 2001, the atmosphere in the company is terrible: it is one of fear, uncertainty and conflict. It is in this context that Silvia has to develop her project and to do this, she must prevail on a number of departments and divisions in the group for help. Yet, since its launch, the TV on ADSL project has given rise to sharp controversy within the group. It quickly became a bone of contention between the manager of the "Landline" division and the manager of the "Internet Access" division. Having had his fingers burnt by bad experiences with similar products, the manager of the "Internet Access" division just does not believe in the concept. In addition, the product relies on the ADSL technology that he considers as his own private domain. Finally, to meet the demands of the regulatory authorities, the initial offer of TV on ADSL has to be separated from a possible Internet access offer, which eliminates any common interest and therefore, any incentive to work together. The "Networks" division, responsible for investment and development in infrastructure is, by and large, lukewarm about the project. TV on ADSL requires specific investment that is costly and considerably increases the financial risk of the operation while the offer, complex to apply and ill-defined, is still a long way from unanimous approval. Only the R&D teams are strongly supportive.

In July 2002, the "enemy" divisions, "Landline" and "Internet Access", merge, causing numerous tensions and resulting in enormous problems for Silvia who loses the support of her hierarchy. In September of the same year, a new CEO is appointed. His first three months of office are to prove to be very dangerous for Silvia's project as its critics choose this period to try and bury it once and for all. Silvia is unable to obtain the resources she needs. She tries as best she can to withstand attempts at intimidation and sabotage. Her direct superior is replaced with scant ceremony by a manager who is against the project and who has no hesitation in saying so. Silvia contemplates "reconversion".

Fortunately, during the autumn, the intervention of the new CEO's adviser is to radically change the situation. She knows the media world very well and promoted an experimental TV on ADSL project when she worked in a ministry. On 1 December, at her initiative, the group signs a contract with a big television channel to carry out a pilot project for video on demand. Silvia's project is now underway and in the spotlight. She has increased resources but has to work twice as hard. A few months later, a general contract is signed with the television channel and the project changes shape: it is no longer a case of doing a pilot but of spreading TV on ADSL across the whole country. The number of people in Silvia's team increases to 30, spread over three sites. Five people from the "Networks" division come and join her team. Their arrival considerably improves the relations between the division and the project team that were previously very difficult. The new CEO and his adviser are strongly involved in the project and closely follow aspects relating to the marketing and management of partnerships. The project's strong visibility galvanises the participants who find it a stimulating challenge and an opportunity to prove their worth. The project advances in leaps and bounds and in December 2003, the roll-down was launched.

Questions:

(1) According to you, is this a case of Spontaneous or Induced Corporate Entrepreneurship?
(2) What goals did Silvia's managers pursue? What benefits did they expect?

(3) What problems and obstacles emerged throughout the process? Could have they been overcome? How?

(5) What were the actual benefits of adopting an entrepreneurial approach to develop the TV on ADSL project? What could have happened if a more traditional approach to innovation had been adopted?

Source: Adapted from Bouchard (2009||C).

Notes

1 www.strategy-business.com/article/8276?gko=8c782 (Accessed 2 August 2017).
2 sloanreview.mit.edu/…/the-four-models-of-corporate-entrepreneur (Accessed 2 August 2017).
3 SBL is a large multinational that provides services to the oil industry. It also develops its own tools and technologies in various laboratories located on three continents.
4 The MEMS technology consists of combining mechanical, electromagnetic, thermic and chemical functions on a 1 mm^2 chip.
5 Among the most detailed and interesting ones, we find Kanter's series on "entrepreneurial vehicles in established firms" (Kanter and Richardson, 1991; Kanter et al., 1991a, 1991b); Bartlett and Mohammed's case (1995) on 3M; Kanter, McGuire and Mohammed's case (1997) on Siemens-Nixdorf; Amabile and Whitney's case (1997) on Procter & Gamble's CNV; Chesbrough and Massaro's case (2001) on Lucent Technologies NVG; and Day et al.'s paper on Nokia's NVO (2001).
6 A 2013 study by Millennial Branding and American Express (http://millennialbranding.com/2013/gen-workplace-expectations-study/) found that "58% of managers are either very willing or extremely willing in supporting entrepreneurial ambitions" (Accessed 2 August 2017).
7 www.businessdictionary.com/article/author/16/ryan-may/ (Accessed 2 August 2017).
8 www.intrapreneur.com/MainPages/History/InnovThruIntra.html (Accessed 2 August 2017).

Corporate Entrepreneurship in the literature: an overview

2

Introduction

Since its emergence in the early 1980s, the topic of Corporate Entrepreneurship has always intrigued scholars and their interest has been growing steadily over the last few decades. When looking at the extant body of literature, however, one observes great heterogeneity of purpose and perspective (Guth and Ginsberg, 1990; Sharma and Chrisman, 1999), which stems in part from the multi-faceted nature of Corporate Entrepreneurship but also from the persistence of unsolved "definitional issues" (Sharma and Chrisman, 1999). In this chapter, we will present the main streams of the scholarly production on Corporate Entrepreneurship and discuss their relations to the fields of Intrapreneurship and Corporate Venturing. We will then review some of the definitions of Corporate Entrepreneurship, pointing at their merits and shortcomings, and clarify our own position.

Corporate Entrepreneurship is a relatively new field of study: it was born in the early 1980s and started to gain momentum in the new millennium to reach a respectable yearly volume of circa 40 academic publications in 2015.[1] Unfortunately, this increase in volume has gone hand in hand with a growing level of fragmentation. Indeed, Corporate Entrepreneurship is now an "umbrella" topic that shelters quite heterogeneous viewpoints and approaches. One stream of the literature defines Corporate Entrepreneurship as something that happens within the firm; that is, an **intra-firm process** resulting in innovation and business creation, another defines Corporate Entrepreneurship as a characteristic of the firm's strategy, which is a **firm-level orientation** towards risk-taking, innovation and responsiveness. The two approaches have very different implications when it comes to selecting research questions and methodologies. But how did such a divide come to be? Let's go back in time and have a look at the genesis of the field.

A bit of history

The first occurrence of the term "Corporate Entrepreneur" in academic literature dates back to a 1974 article by Copulsky and McNulty (1974) which looked at how "corporate entrepreneurs" – employees with an "entrepreneurial personality" – could be identified and better integrated in large companies. The first occurrence of the term "Corporate Entrepreneurship" goes back even further. In a 1969 article, Westfall (1969) explored what organisational factors promote or hinder "Corporate Entrepreneurship"; that is, the desire on the part of corporations "to establish new, need-satisfying business enterprises". But the topic of Corporate Entrepreneurship was firmly established in the realm of academia thanks to a series of articles published by R.A. Burgelman between 1983 and 1984 in which the author describes and analyses the process through which major diversified firms transform R&D activities into new businesses.

Burgelman (1983ASQ) defines Corporate Entrepreneurship as "**the process whereby firms engage in diversification through internal development**". He describes it as a multi-layered process involving "the interlocking strategic activities of managers at different levels of the organization". In another article, Burgelman (1983MS) defines Corporate Entrepreneurship as the process by which autonomous strategies gain organisational acceptance within established firms: "the impetus of Corporate Entrepreneurship lies in the autonomous strategic initiatives of individuals at the organization's operational levels" (Burgelman, 1983MS). The author describes how strategic initiatives emerge, get developed in spite of numerous obstacles, and in some cases, end up contributing to the strategic renewal of the firm. Two years later, Burgelman further elaborated his ideas on Corporate Entrepreneurship in an article on New Venture Divisions (Burgelman, 1985). New Venture Divisions (NVD) are described as "an important innovation aimed at encouraging and facilitating Corporate Entrepreneurship".

Almost concurrently, a group of Canadian scholars (Miller and Friesen, 1982; Mintzberg and Waters, 1982; Miller, 1983) introduced the concept of the "entrepreneurial firm" in a series of ambitious articles studying the relationship between the strategic orientation of firms, their performance and various environmental and organisational factors. For these authors, "entrepreneurial firms", in contrast with "conservative" ones, are characterised by three basic strategic orientations: (1) product innovation; (2) risk taking; and (3) proactiveness. With what environmental and organisational characteristics is an "entrepreneurial orientation" associated? And under what conditions does it result in superior performance? These were questions that nourished a considerable stream of research and publications in the following decade (see Covin and Slevin, 1989; Zahra, 1991; Stopford and Baden-Fuller, 1994; Zahra and Covin, 1995).

This "**entrepreneurial orientation**" stream of research junctured with the field of Corporate Entrepreneurship during the 1990s. Taking stock of the articles they had selected for their special issue on Corporate Entrepreneurship, Guth and Ginsberg stated in their editors' introduction:

> [S]tudies of Corporate Entrepreneurship have tended to focus on internal innovation or venturing but that a broader perspective which involves the creation of new wealth through [. . .] refocusing a business competitively, making major change in marketing or distribution, redirecting product development and reshaping operations should be adopted.
>
> (Guth and Ginsberg, 1990)

In the following years, studies on the entrepreneurial orientation of firms by prominent authors such as Zahra or Covin and Slevin were repositioned within the field of Corporate Entrepreneurship and gave it the dual character that has persisted to this day. The firm-level orientation and the intra-firm process views currently coexist with little, if any, connections at all. Attempts at bridging them have been very few: the contributions of Hornsby et al. (1993), Russell (1999), Brown, Davidsson and Wiklund (2001), Ireland, Covin and Kuratko (2009) and Bouchard and Basso (2011) constitute exceptions.

From early on, **managerial practices aimed at inducing Corporate Entrepreneurship** received the attention of academics: in their "Engines of Progress" series published in *the Journal of Business Venturing* between 1990 and 1991, R.M. Kanter and her co-authors describe and analyse various Corporate Entrepreneurship programmes and structures – "Corporate Entrepreneurship Devices" in our parlance – put in place by well-known companies to "stimulate new ideas and to capture their benefits by channelling them into new products and ventures" (Kanter and Richardson, 1991; Kanter et al., 1991a). Subsequent researchers have explored the relations between innovation projects and the host organisation (Heller, 1999), the functioning principles of Internal Ventures Divisions (Chesbrough, 2000) or the most common management practices aiming at fostering Corporate Entrepreneurship (Bouchard and Fayolle, 2013).

Main research questions and methodologies

Corporate Entrepreneurship remains to this day a polysemous notion, which lacks a commonly accepted definition. Not surprisingly, a significant part of the Corporate Entrepreneurship literature consists in **conceptual articles** that aim at better defining Corporate Entrepreneurship and elaborating models that tie it to relevant internal (organisation, processes) and external (environmental) variables. Among the most relevant contributions in this vein, one can cite contributions by Burgelman (1983MS), Hornsby et al. (1993), Zahra (1993), Lumpkin and Dess (1996), Covin and Miles (1999), Greene, Brush and Hart (1999), Hayton and Kelley (2006) or Ireland, Covin and Kuratko (2009).

The bulk of Corporate Entrepreneurship literature, however, consists of "standard" **quantitative studies** that aim at measuring the statistical correlation between Corporate Entrepreneurship, defined as a firm-level orientation, and some other key variables (performance, features of the environment, features of the organisation, etc.). Various constructs, such as "the entrepreneurial firm" (Miller, 1983), "entrepreneurial management" (Stevenson and Jarillo, 1990) or "entrepreneurial orientation" (Covin and Slevin, 1989), are used to operationalise Corporate Entrepreneurship. The "Entrepreneurial Orientation" (EO) is without discussion the most diffuse of these constructs and the so-called "Covin and Slevin scale" used to measure it, a popular measurement tool (See Box 2.1).

Research on Entrepreneurial Orientation focuses on its definition, its measure and its relationship to various strategic, organisational and environmental factors. More specifically, the discussion of the impact of Entrepreneurial Orientation on performance, in different contexts, for different types of firms, remains a major research topic (Wiklund and Sheperd, 2005; Hughes, Hughes and Morgan, 2007). Researchers have elaborated on a wide array of models: in some, "entrepreneurial orientation" is the only variable explaining performance, in others, it is combined with other variables such as marketing orientation, technological competencies, network competencies and so on. The potential influences of moderating variables such as environmental characteristics, industry life cycle stage and access to financial resources have also been explored.

Box 2.1 Measuring Corporate Entrepreneurship: the Covin and Slevin Scale

Most quantitative studies in the field of Corporate Entrepreneurship use the Covin and Slevin Scale to measure the "Entrepreneurial Orientation" of firms under scrutiny. This scale appeared for the first time in 1989 in Covin and Slevin's article: "Strategic Management of Small Firms in Hostile and Benign Environments". The nine-item scale was part of a questionnaire that managers/owners of SMEs were asked to fill out: it aimed at positioning their strategic posture along a conservative/entrepreneurial continuum – three questions intended to measure the **innovativeness** of their strategy, three questions for its level of **proactivity** and three for its **proclivity for risk** (see questions below). Five of these questions were directly taken from previous studies by Miller and Friesen (1982) and four were original (see Figure 2.1, below).

The Covin and Slevin Scale has been criticised on several accounts: because results depend entirely on the declarations of a single manager, because it mixes current attitudes and past behaviours and because it does not include key entrepreneurial dimensions such as opportunity seizing, for example. Despite its limitations, the Covin and Slevin Scale has gained considerable popularity over the years and continues to be widely used to this day.

There is no lack of conceptual and empirical studies describing and measuring the various factors that contribute to fostering entrepreneurship within established firms, the so-called "**antecedents**" of Corporate Entrepreneurship, and a good synthesis of this literature was elaborated in an article by Ireland, Covin and Kuratko (2009). Extant literature strongly emphasises the important role of **top managers** in inducing Corporate Entrepreneurship (MacMillan, Block and Narasimha, 1986; Kuratko and Montagno, 1989; Morris and Jones, 1999; Garvin, 2002; Herbert and Brazeal, 2004; Ireland, Covin and Kuratko, 2009). The literature also emphasises **autonomy** as one, if not the defining component of Corporate Entrepreneurship (Burgelman, 1983MS; Lumpkin and Dess, 1996; Bouchard and Bos, 2006; Lumpkin, Cogliser and Schneider, 2009). The question of **available resources** and "patient money" is another recurrent theme when discussing the conditions for Corporate Entrepreneurship (Von Hippel, 1977; Sathe, 1985; Kanter, 1985; Burgelman and Sayles, 1986; Sykes and Block, 1989; Garvin, 2002; Kuratko, Hornsby

In general, the top managers of my firm favour . . .		
A strong emphasis on the marketing of tried-and-true products or services	1 to 7	A strong emphasis on R&D, technological leadership, and innovations
How many new lines of products or services has your firm marketed in the past five years (or since its establishment)?		
No new lines of products or services	1 to 7	Very many new lines of products or services
Changes in product or service lines have been mostly of a minor nature	1 to 7	Changes in product or service lines have usually been quite dramatic
In dealing with its competitors, my firm . . .		
Typically responds to actions which competitors initiate	1 to 7	Typically initiates actions to which competitors then respond
Is very seldom the first business to introduce new products/services, administrative techniques, operating technologies, etc.	1 to 7	Is very often the first business to introduce new products/services, administrative techniques, operating technologies, etc.
Typically seeks to avoid competitive clashes, preferring a "live-and-let-live" posture	1 to 7	Typically adopts a very competitive, "undo-the-competitors" posture
In general, the top managers of my firm have . . .		
A strong proclivity for low-risk projects (with normal and certain rates of return)	1 to 7	A strong proclivity for high-risk projects (with chances of very high returns)
In general, the top managers of my firm believe that . . .		
Owing to the nature of the environment, it is best to explore it gradually via cautious, incremental behaviour	1 to 7	Owing to the nature of the environment, bold, wide-ranging acts are necessary to achieve the firm's objectives
When confronted with decision-making situations involving uncertainty, my firm . . .		
Typically adopts a cautious, "wait-and-see" posture in order to minimize the probability of making costly decisions	1 to 7	Typically adopts a bold, aggressive posture in order to maximize the probability of exploiting potential opportunities

Figure 2.1 The Covin and Slevin Scale

Source: Adapted from Covin and Slevin (1989).

and Goldsby, 2004; Ireland, Covin and Kuratko, 2009; Kuratko, Covin and Garrett, 2009). The importance of proper **rewards and incentives** has been underlined by several authors (e.g. Kuratko, Montagno and Hornsby, 1990; Hornsby, Kuratko and Montagno, 1999; Morris and Jones, 1999; Thornberry, 2003; Burgelman, 2005; Hayton, 2005; Brazeal, Schenkel and Azriel, 2008) and their impact on Corporate Entrepreneurship activities has been the object of several studies (Block and Ornati, 1987; Sykes, 1992; Monsen, Patzelt and Saxton, 2010). Another important strand of the literature underlines the multiplicity and heterogeneity of Corporate Entrepreneurship antecedents, viewing each of them as distinct but necessary requirements (Kuratko, Montagno and Hornsby, 1990; Hornsby, Kuratko and Montagno, 1999; Zahra, Jennings, Kuratko, 1999; Garvin, 2002; Herbert and Brazeal, 2004; Brazeal, Schenkel and Azriel, 2008; Ireland, Covin and Kuratko, 2009; Kuratko, Covin and Garrett, 2009; Morris et al., 2009).

Finally, part of the literature consists in single or multiple **case studies** that describe in detail the process that leads to the creation of new activities within established companies and the context in which it unfolds. Quite popular in the early years, thanks to authors such as Burgelman (1983 ASQ), Kanter et al. (1990, 1991a, 1991b), and Stopford and Baden-Fuller (1994), this type of contribution, later exemplified by Badguerahanian and Abetti (1995), Chesbrough (2000), Kuratko, Ireland and Hornsby (2001) and, more recently, De Vita, Sciascia and Alberti (2008) or Bhardwaj, Sushil and Momaya (2011) progressively lost momentum and presently accounts for only a small share of the Corporate Entrepreneurship literature. As a result, the Corporate Entrepreneurship literature body is becoming skewed towards synchronic and quantitative studies with little space left to the detailed description and characterisation of intra-firm, diachronic processes. This is regrettable because, in our opinion, qualitative approaches are particularly well suited in tackling Corporate Entrepreneurship, which remains to this day a complex and elusive organisational process that cannot be fully understood unless the time dimension is taken into account. Figure 2.2, below, synthesises the various strands of the Corporate Entrepreneurship literature.

Two adjacent research fields: Intrapreneurship and Internal Corporate Venturing

The terms "Corporate Entrepreneurship", "Intrapreneurship" and "Internal Corporate Venturing" are often used interchangeably. As we will see in the next section, they are, in fact, almost synonymous and, as a result, the topic of

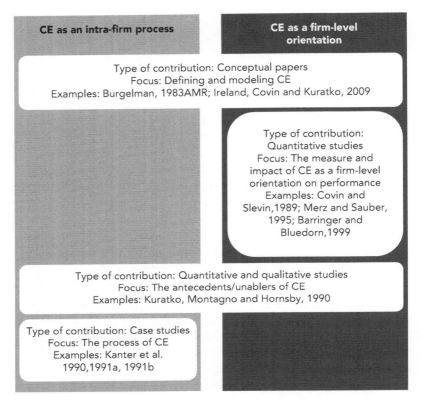

Figure 2.2 A simplified map of Corporate Entrepreneurship literature

Corporate Entrepreneurship cannot be fully embraced without perusing the adjacent fields of Intrapreneurship and Internal Corporate Venturing.

The term "Intrapreneurship" made its first appearance in scholarly journals in 1984. This neologism, which results from the contraction of "intra-company entrepreneurship", has been attributed to the consultant Pinchot (1985, 1987). Because of its self-explanatory nature, the term became quite popular among scholars and managers and a rather large literature grew under this new heading (Morse, 1986; Chisholm, 1987; Luchsinger and Bagby, 1987; Kuratko, Montagno and Hornsby, 1990; Merrifield, 1993; Honig, 2001). Research in Intrapreneurship attempts to answer questions such as: what are the characteristics of the intrapreneur (versus the entrepreneur)? In what context do intrapreneurs thrive? What are the main obstacles to Intrapreneurship in large companies?

Corporate Venturing has been an object of study for several decades now (Von Hippel, 1977; Block and MacMillan, 1993; Chesbrough, 2000; Gompers and Lerner, 2000). Corporate Venturing originally designated the process of new business creation within established firms. Since the 1990s, the term refers to both the **creation** (Internal Venturing) and the **acquisition** of start-ups by established firms (External Venturing). The main research questions in this field revolve around: (1) parent/venture relations and their impact on venture performance; (2) the impact of various characteristics of the environment on venture performance; and (3) characteristics of the venture and the venturing process and their impact on venture performance.

The fields of Corporate Entrepreneurship, Intrapreneurship and (Internal) Corporate Venturing strongly overlap but also have their specificities: the field of (Internal) Corporate Venturing focuses on the creation of new business activities within and by existing firms and on the **strategic** and **financial implications** of this process. The field of Intrapreneurship studies the adoption of entrepreneurial values and behaviours by the employees of well-established firms and focuses on the **impact on innovation, employee behaviour and engagement**. The field of Corporate Entrepreneurship is broader, encompassing the study of new business creation within existing firms as well as the study of firm-level entrepreneurship. It explores the relations of Corporate Entrepreneurship to the **firm's overall performance**, the **antecedents** of Corporate Entrepreneurship and the **process** of Corporate Entrepreneurship both in its spontaneous and "induced" version.

A fact-based research approach

The literature on Corporate Entrepreneurship is characterised by a great heterogeneity of purpose and perspective which stems, in part, from the multifaceted nature of Corporate Entrepreneurship but also from the persistence of unsolved "definitional issues" (Sharma and Chrisman, 1999). The picture becomes even patchier if we focus on Corporate Entrepreneurship, and the related fields of Intrapreneurship and Corporate Venturing. In our opinion, this state of affairs has hindered the process of accumulation and validation of knowledge.

The development of a research field normally alternates between phases of divergence and convergence. Divergence permits exploration, the opening of new doors, experiments in new ways to do research and extending the limits of the research domain. Convergence, however, focuses on establishing the foundations of a field, stabilising key concepts and elaborating

Box 2.2 The field of Corporate Entrepreneurship

Figure 2.3 graphically represents the field of Corporate Entrepreneurship as it evolved since its emergence in the early 1980s:

THE CORPORATE ENTREPRENEURSHIP FIELD

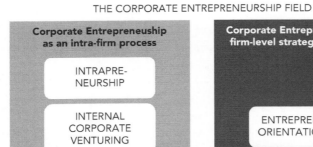
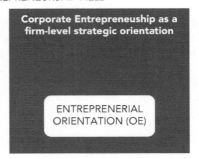

Figure 2.3 The Corporate Entrepreneurship field

The field of Corporate Entrepreneurship is divided in two distinct sub-fields: "Corporate Entrepreneurship as an intra-firm process" and "Corporate Entrepreneurship as a firm-level orientation".

The terms "Intrapreneurship", "Internal Corporate Venturing" and "Corporate Entrepreneurship" are often used interchangeably. As a result, Corporate Entrepreneurship, Intrapreneurship and Internal Corporate Venturing literatures cannot be separated and have to be tackled jointly. The "Corporate Entrepreneurship as a firm-level orientation" sub-field finds its origins in the "entrepreneurial firm" (Miller, 1983) and "entrepreneurial orientation" (Covin and Slevin, 1989) research stream.

and testing constructs. Although there have been periodical "convergence" attempts (Guth and Ginsberg, 1990; Sharma and Chrisman, 1999; Ireland, Covin and Kuratko, 2009), the vast majority of Corporate Entrepreneurship publications fall into the "divergence" category. The amazing diversity of issues addressed, the wide range of labels and notions used to designate the same phenomenon, the exploratory nature of many publications and the large number of new entrants in the field year after year, make Corporate Entrepreneurship a perpetually expanding universe. As a result, in spite of its growing size, the extant literature does not directly address questions of interest to practitioners such as how can Corporate Entrepreneurship be implemented in practice? What are the environmental and organisational conditions for successful implementation? What are the costs and benefits of the various Corporate Entrepreneurship practices? As scholars in Corporate Entrepreneurship in regular contact with executives, the aim of our research has been to try and generate actionable, fact-based knowledge on employee-driven business development/innovation processes and the managerial and organisational practices that can induce them.

Our interest in organisational processes and managerial practices implies the adoption of a qualitative approach based on the accumulation and comparison of multiple case-studies, as only a longitudinal study and a contextualised and comparative approach enables us to grasp complex processes in their entirety. Over the years, we have built a broad base of 30 first-hand and second-hand cases. Together, these cases cover a period of over 30 years (from 1986 to 2013), a variety of geographical locations (North America and several European countries) and a wide array of industries (telecoms, energy, home electronics, IT, fast-moving consumer goods, fashion accessories, air transportation, chemicals, etc.). In the following chapters, we will often refer to facts contained in these cases and to the analyses we performed. A complete list of cases with a short description and bibliographical reference is provided in Appendix 1.

"Definitional issues"

There seems to be as many definitions of Corporate Entrepreneurship as there are scholars. Table 2.1 gives an idea of the array of available definitions.

Looking at the definitions of Intrapreneurship and (Internal) Corporate Venturing, one notes considerable overlap. This confirms that the Corporate Entrepreneurship literature cannot be artificially isolated from Intrapreneurship and Corporate Venturing literatures.

The definition proposed by Sharma and Chrisman (1999) – "Corporate Entrepreneurship is the process whereby an individual or a group of individuals in association with an existing organisation, create a new organisation or instigate renewal or innovation with the organization" – is worth further comment, in our opinion. Their definition is interesting on several accounts: first, it emphasises the role of **individual(s)**, and second, it highlights the existence of an **association** between the individual(s) and the organisation. Finally, it includes, among the outcomes of Corporate Entrepreneurship, not only the creation of new businesses, but **any major innovation** regarding supply and markets, internal processes, systems or the organisation itself.

Table 2.1 Definitions of Corporate Entrepreneurship, Intrapreneurship and Corporate Venturing

Corporate Entrepreneurship

- "Corporate Entrepreneurship refers to the process whereby firms engage in diversification through internal development". (Burgelman, 1983MS)
- "Extending the firm's domain of competence and corresponding opportunity set through internally generated new resource combinations". (Burgelman, 1984)
- "Corporate Entrepreneurship encompasses two types of phenomena and the processes surrounding them: 1) the birth of new businesses within existing organizations and 2) the transformation of organizations through renewal of the key ideas on which they are built i.e., strategic renewal". (Guth and Ginsberg, 1990)
- "The sum of a company's innovation, renewal and venturing efforts". (Zahra, 1993)
- "Together, product innovation, proactiveness, and risk taking capture the essence of Corporate Entrepreneurship". (Zahra and Covin, 1995)
- "An organizational process for transforming individual ideas into collective actions through management". (Chung and Gibbons, 1997)
- "Corporate entrepreneurship include situations where (1) an 'established' organization enters a new business; (2) an individual or individuals champion new product ideas within a corporate context; and (3) an 'entrepreneurial' philosophy permeates an entire organization's outlook and operations". (Covin and Miles, 1999)
- "Corporate Entrepreneurship is the process whereby an individual or a group of individuals in association with an existing organization, create a new organization or instigate renewal or innovation with the organization". (Sharma and Chrisman, 1999)
- "Corporate Entrepreneurship refers to innovative, risk-taking, proactive behaviors pursued at any level and within any area of the firm". (Morris and Kuratko, 2002)

Intrapreneurship

- "Employee initiative from below in the organization to undertake something new; an innovation which is created by subordinates without being asked, expected, or perhaps even given permission by higher management to do so". (Vesper, 1984)
- "Intrapreneurs are . . . 'dreamers who do'; those who take hands-on responsibility for creating innovation of any kind within an organization; they may be the creators or inventors but are always the dreamers who figure out how to turn an idea into a profitable reality". (Pinchot, 1985)

(Continued)

Table 2.1 *continued.*

Intrapreneurship

- "Intrapreneurship refers to a process by which individuals . . . inside organizations pursue opportunities independent of the resources they currently control". (Stevenson and Jarillo 1990)
- "Intrapreneurship refers to emergent behavioral intentions and behaviors that are related to departures from the customary ways of doing business in existing organizations". (Antoncic and Hisrich, 2003)

(Internal) Corporate Venturing

- "Corporate venturing is an activity, which seeks to generate new businesses for the corporation in which it resides through the establishment of external or internal corporate ventures". (Von Hippel, 1977)
- "Corporate Venturing may be defined as the process by which members of an existing firm bring into existence products and markets, which do not currently exist within the repertoire of the firm. This process occurs through transactions (or relationships) with others that take place within different institutional contexts". (Venkataraman, McGrath and MacMillan 1992)
- "A project is a corporate venture when 1) it involves an activity new to the organization, 2) is initiated or conducted internally, 3) involves significantly higher risks of failure and large losses than the organization's base business, 4) will be managed separately at some time during its life, 5) is undertaken for the purpose of increased sales, profit productivity or quality". (Block and McMillan, 1993)

For the previously mentioned reasons, and though it focuses exclusively on the process side of Corporate Entrepreneurship, Sharma and Chrisman's definition has been an important reference in our research.

Corporate Entrepreneurship as an association between individual(s) and organisation: a fruitful hypothesis

Let us consider for a moment the idea of an association between individual(s) and the organisation. Such an association, if it exists, is necessarily asymmetric and complex. Corporate entrepreneurs are required to behave autonomously, yet they remain employees subject to contractual and legal

Table 2.2 Corporate Entrepreneurship as an association between individual(s) and their organisation

	Individual(s)	The organisation
What Corporate Entrepreneurship means for . . .	An innovation/development approach suited to certain projects in given situations.	
	A stimulating, demanding and sometimes risky journey	A management tool that allows improvement in certain aspects of the firm's performance
Main contributions of . . .	Engagement, creativity, talent, expertise, influence, own network resources	Resources, expertise, strategic framework, performance indicators, methods, incentives, best practices/examples of success, support processes
Respective roles of . . .	Personally committed to the success of, and identified to, a project pursued on behalf of the organisation	Committed to encourage, guide, assess and support the individuals whose projects meet certain criteria

obligations, including that of acting for the benefit of their employer. The organisation, on its side, "delegates" certain tasks and transfers certain risks to corporate entrepreneurs, but it also constitutes their nurturing milieu and acts as the judge of their performance. Table 2.2 attempts to clarify the respective position and roles of the two "associates".

From the standpoint of the individual, being associated to an organisation in the pursuit of a venture has pros and cons. Thanks to their insiders' status, corporate entrepreneurs have access to resources and expertise of all kinds. But corporate entrepreneurs have to trade some of their autonomy in exchange for the safety net and resources provided by the organisation. To get the support of internal stakeholders, they have to compromise on certain features of their project, running the risk of depriving it of its originality. They might sometimes feel that their time would be better spent approaching prospective clients than doing politics. They might also come to realise that the organisation is as much a hindrance as a support and, in the case of success, they will have to share the gains with the organisation. On the other hand, corporate entrepreneurs get paid monthly and know that they can fall back on their regular activities in case of failure.

Box 2.3 Independent entrepreneur or corporate entrepreneur?

It is not uncommon for researchers and engineers working in the labs of high-tech firms to consider resigning in order to try and commercialise a promising invention. However, commercialising their invention inside the company is an option they definitely have to take into consideration before deciding to fly with their own wings. How should they go about deciding to go alone or remaining an employee?

The first question they must ask themselves is: "Can my company be a good, reliable partner?" If the organisation does not have much to offer in financial and expertise terms, if there are no potential champions for their project and if the project does not require resources or competencies that are unique to the company, the best choice might be to leave. Otherwise, the advantages and disadvantages of both options should be weighed carefully:

Potential advantages of the Corporate Entrepreneurship option are the following:

– Easier access to funding and critical expertise/resources (especially if the employee knows the organisation well).
– No time wasted in administrative tasks tied to creating a company, hiring and managing employees on a daily basis.
– Regular income and limited financial risk.

But there are also some drawbacks:

– Lots of time spent managing "interfaces": selling the project internally, preventing sabotage, finding internal sponsors and building alliances, getting approvals and resources. This can be frustrating and time-consuming.
– The pressures exercised by the organisation's various constituencies can denature the initial project and strip it of his innovative content.
– Successful corporate entrepreneurs appropriate – at best – only a small part of the value they have created.

In summary

☐ The field of Corporate Entrepreneurship was born in the early 1980s with the seminal publications of R.A. Burgelman.

☐ It is an "umbrella" field that shelters heterogeneous strands of research. One strand defines Corporate Entrepreneurship as something that happens within the firm; that is, an **intra-firm process** resulting in innovation and business creation, another defines Corporate Entrepreneurship as a characteristic of the firm's strategy, which is a **firm-level orientation** towards risk-taking, innovativeness and proactiveness.

☐ The terms "Corporate Entrepreneurship", "Intrapreneurship" and "Internal Corporate Venturing" are almost synonymous and often used interchangeably: as a result, the topic of Corporate Entrepreneurship cannot be fully apprehended without exploring the adjacent fields of Intrapreneurship and Internal Corporate Venturing.

☐ The Corporate Entrepreneurship literature is dominated by conceptual contributions and quantitative studies mobilising the Entrepreneurial Orientation construct. Qualitative research relying on the diachronic observation of the processes at play, in single or multiple case studies, have seen their weight decline over time.

☐ There seems to exist as many definitions of Corporate Entrepreneurship as there are scholars. Our preference goes to the two following definitions:

  ○ "Corporate entrepreneurship include situations where (1) an 'established' organization enters a new business; (2) an individual or individuals champion new product ideas within a corporate context; and (3) an 'entrepreneurial' philosophy permeates an entire organization's outlook and operations". (Covin and Miles, 1999)

  ○ "Corporate Entrepreneurship is the process whereby an individual or a group of individuals in association with an existing organization, create a new organization or instigate renewal or innovation with the organization". (Sharma and Chrisman, 1999)

☐ Covin and Miles' definition is comprehensive. Sharma and Chrisman's definition is interesting on several accounts: first, it emphasises the role of **individuals**, and second, it highlights the existence of an **association** between the individual(s) and the organisation. Finally, it includes, among the outcomes of Corporate Entrepreneurship, not only the creation of new businesses, but **any major innovation** regarding supply and markets, internal processes, systems or the organisation itself.

To go further

In order to go further and apply some of the conceptual frameworks presented in this chapter, read Chapter 3: "Corporate Entrepreneurship at L'Oréal: an integrative case study" and answer the questions listed at the end of the chapter.

Note

1 Source: Proquest – Academic papers.

Corporate Entrepreneurship at L'Oréal: an integrative case study

3

For this *Handbook*, our choice has been to put more emphasis on Corporate Entrepreneurship as an **internal process** rather than as a **firm-level orientation** (cf. Chapter 2). Part 2 of this book is indeed dedicated to describing and analysing in detail such processes. We have also decided to emphasise the deliberate actions and devices adopted by companies in order to favour the Corporate Entrepreneurship process. Part 3 of this book consists of a thorough account and analysis of how companies encourage Corporate Entrepreneurship in practice and the managerial and organisational tools they put in place to do so.

To ensure that **Corporate Entrepreneurship as a firm-level orientation** is given adequate attention, and that the reader gets exposed to the example of a company with a strong and deeply ingrained **entrepreneurial culture**, resulting from the accumulation over decades of "pro-entrepreneurial" management decisions and practices, we conclude this first, exploratory part with a case study on L'Oréal.[1]

This case should also be used as a study assignment to integrate and deepen the notions presented in the previous chapter.

The case *per se* is preceded by an overview of some key conceptual constructs related to Corporate Entrepreneurship as a firm-level orientation. It is followed by a list of questions that require the reader to relate these constructs to the facts described in the case and perform an in-depth analysis of the factors – environmental, organisational, managerial and procedural – that have contributed to L'Oréal's strong entrepreneurial orientation and impressive success over time.

Firm-level Corporate Entrepreneurship: the key constructs

We have chosen to focus on the contribution of three key authors to provide the reader with the conceptual toolkit needed to analyse the L'Oréal integrative case:

- Miller and Friesen (1982) and Miller (1983) were the first to observe the "entrepreneurial firm" and who showed that entrepreneurship manifests itself differently in distinct organisational configurations.
- Covin and Slevin (1988, 1989) who introduced the concept of entrepreneurial orientation and proposed a scale to measure its intensity.
- Stevenson and Gumpert (1985), Stevenson and Jarillo (1990) who developed an approach to entrepreneurial management that distinguishes firms and managers that have an entrepreneurial culture from firms and managers that have an administrative culture.

Miller's construct (1983): the entrepreneurial firm

For Miller (1983), "An entrepreneurial firm is one that engages in product market innovation, undertakes somewhat risky ventures, and is first to come up with proactive innovations, beating competitors to the punch". In some ways, organisational entrepreneurship is conceptualised as a combination of three variables: innovativeness, risk-taking and proactivity, or, as the writer himself puts it: "We can tentatively view entrepreneurship as a composite weighting of these three variables". The definition of the "entrepreneurial firm" offered by Miller (1983) and the three variables upon which it is constructed has constituted a reference for all future works on this subject and later gave rise to the concept of "entrepreneurial orientation". Miller (1983) shows that entrepreneurship and the factors that influence it vary with the different types of organisational configurations, which themselves depend on contingency factors and a number of other factors relating to the personality of managers, structure, strategy and organisation. It seems that in "simple" organisational configurations, essentially small and medium-sized businesses evolving in homogeneous environments and directed by people who are also the owners, where power is centralised and strategies are implicit, entrepreneurship depends directly on the vision of the managers. In this type of organisation, entrepreneurship is mainly influenced by the manager and his or her personality (internal locus of control), power (centralisation of decision making) and knowledge (of markets, products and technologies) from which innovative ideas may emerge. But this power does not allow him or her to grasp all the difficulties relating to entrepreneurship, particularly in terms of the environment and structure. In other, "more planned" organisational configurations, which can be characterised by the stability and predictability of their environment, the quality of their planning and control systems and the efficiency of their functioning, it is the strategies, products and markets, clearly identified and integrated, that will influence entrepreneurship. Finally, in "organic" organisational configurations, characterised by their dynamic and complex environment, the question of adapting to new conditions in a changing environment will be decisive. In this type of organisation, entrepreneurship is largely determined by the environment and the structure of the firm via the options of decentralised authority, recourse to expert opinion and internal communication. Actions relating to structure aim to adapt and above all, to innovate.

The entrepreneurial processes thus manifest in distinct ways in different contexts: risk-taking will be decisive in small and medium-sized businesses, as will the capacity for innovation in the organic company and proactiveness in the large bureaucratic company.

Covin and Slevin's construct (1989): entrepreneurial orientation

Most quantitative studies in the field of Corporate Entrepreneurship use the Covin and Slevin Scale to measure the "entrepreneurial orientation" of firms under scrutiny (see Figure 3.1). This scale appeared for the first time in 1989 in Covin and Slevin's article: "Strategic Management of Small Firms in Hostile and Benign Environments". The nine-item scale was part of a questionnaire that managers/owners of manufacturing sector SMEs were asked to fill out: it aimed at positioning their strategic posture along a conservative/entrepreneurial continuum. Three questions were intended to measure the **innovativeness** of their strategy, its level of **proactivity** and its **risk-taking** (see the questions listed at the end). Five of these questions were directly taken from previous studies by Miller and Friesen (1982) and four were additions of the authors.

The Covin and Slevin scale has been criticised on several accounts: because results depend entirely on the declarations of a single manager, because it mixes current attitudes and past behaviours and because it does not include key entrepreneurial dimensions such as opportunity-seizing, for example.

In general, the top managers of my firm favour . . .		
A strong emphasis on the marketing of tried-and-true products or services	1 to 7	A strong emphasis on R&D, technological leadership, and innovations
How many new lines of products or services has your firm marketed in the past five years (or since its establishment)?		
No new lines of products or services	1 to 7	Very many new lines of products or services
Changes in product or service lines have been mostly of a minor nature	1 to 7	Changes in product or service lines have usually been quite dramatic
In dealing with its competitors, my firm . . .		
Typically responds to actions which competitors initiate	1 to 7	Typically initiates actions to which competitors then respond
Is very seldom the first business to introduce new products/services, administrative techniques, operating technologies, etc.	1 to 7	Is very often the first business to introduce new products/services, administrative techniques, operating technologies, etc.
Typically seeks to avoid competitive clashes, preferring a "live-and-let-live" posture	1 to 7	Typically adopts a very competitive, "undo-the-competitors" posture
In general, the top managers of my firm have . . .		
A strong proclivity for low-risk projects (with normal and certain rates of return)	1 to 7	A strong proclivity for high-risk projects (with chances of very high returns)
In general, the top managers of my firm believe that . . .		
Owing to the nature of the environment, it is best to explore it gradually via cautious, incremental behaviour	1 to 7	Owing to the nature of the environment, bold, wide-ranging acts are necessary to achieve the firm's objectives
When confronted with decision-making situations involving uncertainty, my firm		
Typically adopts a cautious, "wait-and-see" posture in order to minimize the probability of making costly decisions	1 to 7	Typically adopts a bold, aggressive posture in order to maximize the probability of exploiting potential opportunities

Figure 3.1 The Covin and Slevin Scale

Source: Adapted from Covin and Slevin (1989).

In spite of its limitations, the Covin and Slevin scale has gained considerable popularity over the years and continues to be widely used to this day. By focusing on three well-established dimensions of entrepreneurship; that is, innovativeness, proactivity and risk-taking, it can constitute a useful tool for quickly assessing the entrepreneurial orientation of a firm at a given point of time.

Stevenson's construct (1985, 1990): entrepreneurial management

For Stevenson and Jarillo (1990, p. 23), "An entrepreneurial organization is that which pursues opportunities, regardless of resources currently controlled". Stevenson (2000), who came up with this concept, offers a model that contrasts a classic vision of management with an entrepreneurial vision. Non-entrepreneurial organisations are built largely on a system of planning and control centred on resources owned, whereas in entrepreneurial organisations, new resources are developed through a strong orientation towards business opportunities, which leads to the launch of new products, new technologies and entry to new markets. For Stevenson and Gumpert (1985), a company's culture is characterised by its level of entrepreneurial focus depending on its position on a continuum constructed using five managerial dimensions: strategic orientation, commitment to seize opportunities, commitment (of resources) during the process, control of resources and management structure (see Table 3.1).

What emerges from these works is that entrepreneurial behaviour, here meaning the creation of a new product or service within a company, depends on unique processes and on singular structural and organisational factors, which facilitate or inhibit its occurrence. The case study that follows shows many examples of these unique processes and singular factors.

Corporate Entrepreneurship at L'Oréal

Overview of the company's history

L'Oréal, a company that in 2016 reported a turnover of €25.8 billion, employed 89,300 people and was present in 140 countries (L'Oréal 2016 Annual Report), was created in 1907 by a young chemist, Eugène Schueller. It claims to have a culture of innovation that aims not so much to develop "inventions" that can disrupt, as to constantly modernise families of cosmetic products spread across

Table 3.1 The entrepreneurial culture versus the administrative culture (Stevenson and Gumpert, 1985)

	Entrepreneurial culture	Administrative culture
Strategic orientation	Driven by perception of opportunities	Driven by control of resources
Commitment to seizing opportunities	Revolutionary, with short duration	Evolutionary, with long duration
Commitment of resources	Many stages, with minimal exposure at each stage	A single stage with complete commitment of decisions
Control of resources	Episodic use or rent of required resources	Ownership or employment of required resources
Management structure	Flat with multiple informal networks	Hierarchy

Source: Adapted from Stevenson and Gumpert (1985).

a portfolio of major brands that are world renowned (L'Oréal Paris, Garnier, Maybelline, Vichy, Ralph Lauren, Helena Rubinstein, etc.).

Since its creation, L'Oréal has placed importance on the growth of its activities and turnover. Although during the 1960s and the beginning of the 1970s, under the impetus of François Dalle, L'Oréal grew partly through acquisitions (Vichy, Biotherm, Garnier, Lancôme, Guy Laroche, Gemey, Laboratoires Roja), the group then focused on internal growth until the end of his directorship: "Our development is basically founded on knowledge built up in the business and we have only undertaken acquisitions where our know-how would allow them to be fruitful" (Dalle, 2001, p. 383). With the arrival of Lindsay Owen-Jones, in 1988, L'Oréal revived external growth. This was given considerable thought, with a view to taking market share in certain countries – notably in the USA, where L'Oréal successively acquired Helena Rubinstein in 1988, Maybelline in 1996, Soft Sheen in 1998 and Carson in 2000 on the "ethnic" products market. Whilst the group has always sought to maintain its historical position in Europe, this market today represents less than half its turnover. The USA now accounts for 30 per cent of sales, and opportunities in the years to come seem to be linked to the development of emergent markets in which L'Oréal created subsidiaries throughout the 1990s. The company is fully committed to a strategy that aims for global distribution of a limited number of well-known cosmetic product ranges.

Key characteristics of organisational configuration

L'Oréal operates in the cosmetics industry; its environment is globalised, dynamic and complex. The growth potential for the sector is not the same in all geographical regions. In developed countries (Western Europe, USA and Japan), the industry's growth rate is slightly higher than the GDP, whereas in developing countries, it is above 8 per cent (Collin and Rouach, 2009). The complexity of the environment is linked to the type of competitive system, which is specialised and requires the successful combination of two logics that would appear contradictory: high volumes to benefit from economies of scale and differentiation of products with the objective of gaining high market share through a host of niche markets (Collin and Rouach, 2009). In this type of environment, the capacity for innovation is generally an essential competitive advantage.

If we refer to the types of configurations identified by Miller (1983), the one that seems to apply best to L'Oréal today is the "organic" configuration. Organic configurations do well in dynamic environments, in which questions of adaptation to change, especially innovation, are key. To respond to this, companies can act on their structures in order to make them more proactive, particularly through decentralisation and internal communication. More specifically, to adapt to the conditions of a changing environment, L'Oréal has used the personalities of its managers, culture and management. The company also benefitted from the great stability of its governance and cooperation between the majority shareholder (descendants of Eugène Schueller) and its managers. One of the effects of this has been to strengthen, over time, the strategic and managerial continuity, as we will see in the next part of our development.

Exceptional managers

L'Oréal has had just four directors in a little over a century of business: the founder Eugène Schueller, François Dalle, Charles Zviak and Lindsay Owen-Jones (Marseille, 2009). The central character in this long history is probably François Dalle. He was recruited by Eugène Schueller in 1948 and made Director of L'Oréal. François Dalle also recruited Lindsay Owen-Jones, another of the company's great characters (Collin and Rouach, 2009) and would choose, when the time came, his two successors. The contribution of Eugène Schueller can be analysed on two levels. First, he was the person who, through his training as a chemist and scientific education, gave so much importance to research and innovation within the company. He also shaped L'Oréal's strong internal culture by instituting discussions and meetings on short-term challenges (new projects) and medium-term goals (the future of the company and/or sector). But it was François Dalle who, over 36 years at the helm, would progressively write L'Oréal's official biography. Eugène Schueller said of him at the end of his life: "I am a man of small and medium-sized companies, but Dalle is a man of great perspectives, he is the one who will make L'Oréal" (Marseille, 2009, p. 147). His original actions and daring gambles would lay down, little by little, the reference points for managerial actions within the company. By way of example, we might take the launch, in 1962, of Elnett hairspray, which, with its much talked about advertising, continues to dominate the market 50 years later (Marseille, 2009, pp. 162–168). Elnett was an unexpected success and became one of the myths of the great L'Oréal brand. François Dalle was not an ordinary company head and always defended strong ideas that showed an entrepreneurial mindset, particularly by asking uncomfortable questions, rather than just accepting quiet satisfaction with things already in place: "In order to progress, there needed to be shocks and in order to have shocks, confrontations needed to be organised. I got on with it, notably by re-naming the meeting room of our headquarters 'the confrontation room'" (François Dalle, quoted in Collin and Rouach, 2009, p. 39).

In the company's history, François Dalle is certainly the one who most embodies the independent entrepreneur and risk-taker who creates companies. He developed L'Oréal, particularly in terms of its international activities, to the point where by the time of his departure, it had become the largest international cosmetics group.

Lindsay Owen-Jones was both a man of continuity and disruption (Marseille, 2009). He inherited and was the guardian of the group's key reference points (Collin and Rouach, 2009), but he also fostered the ability to adapt to changes over the years. Lindsay Owen-Jones was the manager of decentralisation, setting up a veritable cult of the informal and culture of internal competition and emulation between individuals, brands and units. From this point of view, he seems to have been the one who managed L'Oréal's transition towards the organic configuration, which characterises the company today. In his role as Director, he showed a keen sense of anticipation, identifying emerging trends in the African and Asian markets (Collin and Rouach, 2009).

A culture oriented towards entrepreneurship

The culture of L'Oréal is very much centred on the behaviour of individuals and their ability to undertake projects and bring them to fruition (Collin and Rouach, 2009). The main values of the company are innovation, informal operation and autonomy. The transmission of L'Oréal's culture, particularly to new recruits, relies on constant reminders of the great stories of its founders and examples of successes that contributed to the group's construction. These edifying stories have the effect of coordinating the ways of thinking and acting by offering a system of precise reference points. The company uses entrepreneurial discourse full of references to the initiatives and actions of its emblematic managers, who are depicted as models from whom one takes inspiration. L'Oréal has its own language, which reflects these common cultural references. This verbal code is expressed through a series of slogans and messages, repeated and broadcast both inside and outside the company. Here are some examples: "At L'Oréal, you can be a boss before you reach the age of 30"; "The best people are those who can disrupt"; "Staff must be able to take on several projects at once and keep all the plates spinning". These quotes really function as principles for action in the company and legitimise behaviour that would certainly be unacceptable in other organisations. For example, the adage, "Do, un-do to do better" has for a long time allowed the last-minute, and therefore costly, reconsideration of investments already planned to be justified.

Characterised by reverence for the sense of initiative and individual responsibility, the group's culture has influenced the organisation, which is characterised by a low degree of formalisation of processes and procedures. As François Dalle wrote:

> [T]he whole company must actually be brought into a sort of Brownian movement. I never hesitated in shaking up structures in order to organise the disorder, because a certain amount of disorder is essential for creation... Accept what needs to be done in order to better un-do... , this basically means renouncing, to a great extent, the comfort of acquired positions in an organisational structure.
>
> (Dalle, 2001, p. 268)

Nonetheless, at L'Oréal, disorder is far from anarchy and follows a method in which mental preparation plays a part. There is a real kind of cultural modelling, which is explicitly sought and constitutes one of the company's strengths.

A management system for entrepreneurial skills

Regarding management of human resources, L'Oréal appears atypical in many ways. The company recruits new staff members according to criteria that favours candidates with sensitivity, intuition, imagination, taste for autonomy and clear potential for successful development projects – in other words, entrepreneurs in the making. At L'Oréal, they believe that these qualities can only be revealed through action, which explains why the company tries to give young managers missions that are likely to involve market reaction. From then on, it is out in the field that they earn their stripes. François Dalle always believed that the recruitment of entrepreneurial profiles was a priority for L'Oréal: "This [i.e. the growth of L'Oréal] was the work of entrepreneurs, in the full sense of the term, to whom I wish to pay particular respect" (Dalle, 2001, p. 238).

The high level of importance attached to human resource management can be seen in the following comments from François Dalle:

> Our stance of openness to the realities of life has shaped the recruitment and training policies of our managers. I've always ensured that this pioneering attitude, the spirit of the road and the workshop, has prevailed over the spirit of the office management. I believe that this requirement is particularly important today for two reasons. It's in places that things are sold and consumed that progress is born; it's in the factories, shops, and homes rather than in the computer-cave. It's in those same places that solidarity is strengthened.
>
> (Dalle, 2001, p. 258)

Career evolution takes place through successive achievements and the elected managers must have been able to show a real ability to "maintain constant energy and manage an activity in an autonomous way" over the course of their previous positions.

But one of the distinctive characteristics of people management, which, in fact, emulates a certain sort of entrepreneurial behaviour, is competition. Every individual is encouraged to take initiatives, to innovate, but he or she must be able to defend ideas and projects in a competitive environment where only the best performers will be rewarded.

As well as the demand for strong devotion to the company's cause, the organisation promotes a certain amount of acceptance of failure, which can be seen, in particular, in the promise of a second chance given to talented staff members who did not manage to successfully conclude an initiative or project which satisfied the requirements of a mission. François Dalle also sets out his position on this question:

> Without mistakes, no change is possible, or evolution or progress. . . the role of the manager is to help commit to correcting them. I've spent

a good part of my career doing this and I have never failed to evoke, on these occasions, the errors that I made myself. It goes to show that authority, the source of power, comes not just from success, but also from the mistakes that you have known how to admit and correct.

(Dalle, 2001, p. 381)

Entrepreneurial processes

Ability to innovate and orientation towards opportunities

L'Oréal has increased new product launches, which have often found success in markets due to their perceived quality in comparison to competitor products. Before L'Oréal entered the deodorant market in France, this underdeveloped market was dominated by the unsophisticated brand "Odorono". L'Oréal launched the Printil brand and then added deodorants to its cosmetic lines of Mennen, Biotherm, Vichy and Obao, and then to its perfume lines. The lesson L'Oréal learnt from its entry into the French deodorant market is that you must know how to move beyond the realities of the moment and take risks by innovating in the exploration of new territories (Marseille, 2009).

But the attention that L'Oréal pays to the expectations of consumers also legitimises a policy of innovation favouring incremental innovations that involves constant modernisation of existing ranges of cosmetic products. L'Oréal's activities take place within a highly competitive environment and this type of innovation relies on a high level of R&D. In 2008, L'Oréal created an innovation department answering directly to the Director Jean-Paul Agon. The principal objective assigned to this unit is to discover and identify new opportunities, both in terms of customers' expectations and scientific and technological discoveries. L'Oréal holds around 20,000 patents and registers almost 500 per year. The company allocates more than three per cent of the group's total turnover to R&D annually (Collin and Rouach, 2009). The systematic distribution of innovations according to the different channels, characteristics and countries allows the R&D costs to be absorbed and to cover markets with a reactivity that slows down and limits the market penetration of competitor products. In terms of research, L'Oréal works with laboratories around the world (for example, INSERM and the CNRS in France) and favours permanent connections with the best researchers in its specialist research areas.

But the innovation at the heart of the company does not only concern the launch of new products and improvement of existing ranges. As the past 40 years demonstrate, L'Oréal has also innovated by taking up positions in unknown markets, mostly in foreign countries. François Dalle summarises very well their point of view:

> Because we are convinced, at L'Oréal, that you only find on a market what you have put there, I think we can say that we are market openers. But it's never easy, because the initiative always comes up against resistance from many staff members. Some are obsessed by analyses of what already exists and incapable of sensing possible openings and even go as far as to deny that they exist. Others shrink away from risks: the manager's mind-set wins against the business mind-set. My role, as the head of L'Oréal, was to prevail against such resistance.
>
> (Dalle, 2001, p. 278)

Pro-activeness and commitment to opportunities

A depth of knowledge regarding the habits and preferences of their different consumers together with very close teamwork between the marketing and R&D departments allows L'Oréal to develop products that are perfectly suited to the needs of the market. Intimate knowledge of their clients has always been one of the company's key concerns: "Discovering unsatisfied needs and needs that are still to be satisfied, constantly opening markets to new consumers, worrying about their opinions of our products, these were my concerns at any given moment" (Dalle, 2001, p. 259). L'Oréal is constantly looking to discover new niches, consumers' special needs for which no products currently exist. To achieve this, the group has put in place different kinds of monitoring systems: commercial, competitive, political, social and technological. It is particularly these monitoring initiatives that allowed them, in the mid-1990s, to notice that there were very few products aimed at Asian skin types (Collin and Rouach, 2009). L'Oréal has also introduced innovative monitoring practices, for example, by installing the "feedback report" for new employees. Every researcher who works abroad is asked to provide feedback on anything that surprised or confused them, rather than simply reporting the facts or interpretations of the facts in a conventional manner. This practice encourages the researcher to ask questions about how they interact with the environment and to develop observation and listening skills and curiosity. François Dalle was the one who came up with the feedback report (cf. Dalle, 1990).

The company's pro-activeness comes as much from its organisation as human resource management. Power is very decentralised and working relationships remain quite informal. Unlike most large companies, L'Oréal appears more like a group of SMEs (subsidiaries, businesses, departments, etc.), which deals with suppliers of similar size as equals. Whilst industrial purchasing is centralised, those relating to marketing are entirely decentralised. Every business or subsidiary is responsible for its own purchasing policy. This can be explained by the fact that within the company there is a fear of large systems, which may, of course, have advantages for economies of scale but which can also become difficult to manage and end in the company losing flexibility and reactivity. L'Oréal therefore accepts the commercial risk of having a host of small businesses and SMEs as suppliers. These companies are selected on quality criteria, price and reactivity and when a supplier joins the network, L'Oréal tries to build long-lasting win–win relationships with them.

To go further: in-depth case analysis

Your task is to try and identify the various factors and processes that have facilitated (or inhibited) the emergence and consolidation of L'Oréal's strong entrepreneurial orientation, using the conceptual frameworks presented in the first section of this chapter.

(1) Referring yourself to the Covin and Slevin entrepreneurial orientation scale, try to measure L'Oréal's degree of Innovativeness, Responsiveness and Risk-taking. When appropriate, establish distinctions between the three "eras" ("Schueller era", "Dalle era" and "Owen-Jones era").
(2) Referring yourself to Miller's configurational model of the entrepreneurial firm, describe the main environmental and internal variables that have had an impact on L'Oréal's entrepreneurial orientation and formulate hypotheses regarding their impact on Innovativeness, Responsiveness and Risk-taking. When appropriate, establish distinctions between the three "eras" ("Schueller era", "Dalle era" and "Owen-Jones era").

Variables mentioned by Miller (1983) that you might want to consider:[2]

- Size of the company
- Locus of control of the top managers (inner-directed / other directed)
- Type of environment (dynamism, heterogeneity, hostility)
- Organisation (intensity of scanning activity, intensity of control activity, intensity of communication, availability of resources, level of centralisation, technocratisation, specialisation, integration)
- Decision-making processes (importance of systematic analysis, futurity, explicitness of product-market strategy, strategic integration)

(3)   Referring yourself to Stevenson and Gumpert's (1985) entrepreneurial management model, try to position L'Oréal on an Entrepreneurial/Administrative continuum. When appropriate, establish distinctions between the three "eras" ("Schueller era", "Dalle era" and "Owen-Jones era").

(4)   What conclusions can you draw from the above analyses? Do you think that some key factors explaining L'Oréal's strong entrepreneurial orientation are not accounted for by the proposed conceptual constructs?

(5)   Entrepreneurial organisations actively fight the ailments associated with "growing big". According to you, what is the successful recipe of L'Oréal? What levers does it emphasise and how?

Notes

1   Part of this chapter is adapted from earlier work by the authors (Fayolle, Basso and Legrain, 2008).

2   To understand the precise meaning of the listed variables, read in full the articles by Miller and Friesen (1982) and Miller (1983).

Part 2

Understanding the Corporate Entrepreneurship process

Corporate Entrepreneurship can be simply defined as "entrepreneurship within the corporation": but is this basic definition good enough? To answer this question, one needs to carefully observe the Corporate Entrepreneurship process as it unfolds in practice, using (Independent) Entrepreneurship as a benchmark. The second part of this book, "Understanding the Corporate Entrepreneurship process", includes:

* A description of the main stages of the Corporate Entrepreneurship process, underlining its specificities (Chapter 4).
* A look at team dynamics and management as an integral and critical part of the Corporate Entrepreneurship process (Chapter 5).

Corporate Entrepreneurship: a specific process? **4**

Introduction

One of the central theses of this *Handbook* is that the Corporate Entrepreneurship process and the (Independent) Entrepreneurship process have many similarities but that it would be wrong and even perilous to equate them. This might lead to erroneous perceptions and undesirable consequences for those in charge of implementing and managing Corporate Entrepreneurship.

Whatever autonomy they enjoy, energy they deploy and calculated risk they take, corporate entrepreneurs remain employees who work for a company and get a pay cheque at the end of the month. Corporate entrepreneurs do not choose the culture of the organisation they work for and have to constantly negotiate their autonomy and resources with that organisation. As a result, they dedicate a lot of time and energy to what we call "managing interfaces": getting support from various stakeholders, neutralising potential opponents, convincing their boss and sponsors that the project is worthwhile, asking help from their colleagues, reporting to their hierarchy and so on. Corporate entrepreneurs always fight on two fronts and must have a double set of competencies: they must be able to deal with the external market and its uncertainties and, at the same time, they have to manage a diverse set of "internal clients". This dual challenge has implications at all stages of the Corporate Entrepreneurship process, as will now be shown.

The New Venture Development process

The process of New Venture Development (NVD) constitutes the core of both Entrepreneurship and Corporate Entrepreneurship.[1] This process "involves all functions, actions and activities associated with perceiving opportunities and creating organisations to pursue them" (Bygrave and Hofer, 1991). It includes the development of a product or service, obtaining resources, designing organisations and the development of strategies to exploit opportunities (Shane, 2003, p. 10).

The NVD process unfolds according to a sequence that remains globally invariant but that is described in different terms and cut in different "chunks" according to what dimension of the process the authors wish to emphasise. Galbraith's New Venture model (1983), for example, focuses on the product/ activity development dimension and its various steps correspond to product/ activity growth stages (Figure 4.1).

In his New Venture model, Gartner (1985) goes beyond product/activity development stages to include some of the key strategic and organisational challenges that arise as entrepreneurs move ahead in the development process (Figure 4.2).

The NVD model proposed by www.startupcommons.org encompasses both the challenges facing entrepreneurs and the activities they need to perform as the venture progresses. The model describes the challenges as a series of "fits" that need to be established: the first one is a "problem-solution fit",

Figure 4.1 Galbraith's New Venture Development model (1983)

Source: Adapted from Galbraith (1983).

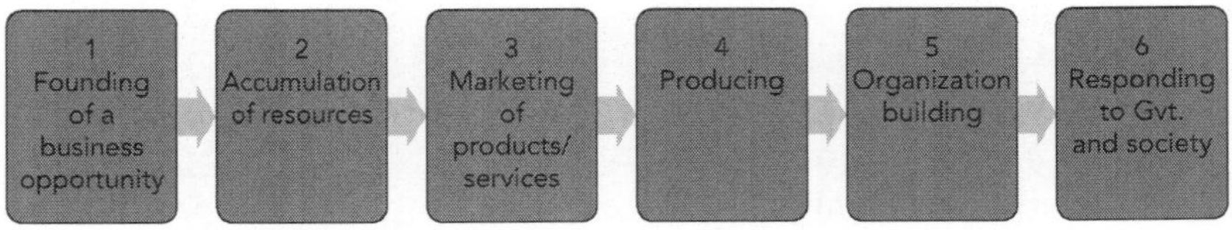

Figure 4.2 Gartner's New Venture model (1985)

Source: Adapted from Gartner (1985).

the second a "vision-founder fit", then a "product-market fit" and so on. In parallel, the key activities of developers evolve from "ideating" to "concepting" to "committing" (which, in this model, constitutes the real starting point of the venturing process), to "validating", "scaling" and "establishing" (Figure 4.3).

Corporate Venture Development models

When NVD takes place in a corporate context, additional variables and dynamics have to be factored in. As mentioned earlier, corporate entrepreneurs dedicate a lot of time and energy to "managing interfaces", be they hierarchical or institutional (Venkataraman, McGrath and MacMillan, 1992), vertical or horizontal. The Corporate Entrepreneurship process, therefore, involves a combination of venture development stages and interface management stages.

Burgelman's Corporate Venture Development model (1983 ASQ) examines the role played by three different categories of corporate actors and describes how this role varies at each stage of the process (see Figure 4.4). "Corporate management" sets the directions for new ventures, monitors the innovation process and rewards success. "Middle management" manages the new ventures portfolio and acts as the "organisational champion" of ventures. Finally, at the bottom of the pyramid, "Venture leaders" generate ideas, ensure the technological and market development of individual ventures and challenge, when necessary, the directions set by "corporate management".

On top of the two **core** processes of "definition" (idea generation; product definition) and "impetus" (market and technology building), Burgelman identifies two **overlaying** processes, which are specific to the corporate context. "Structural context" processes consist of ensuring that all "lower level" activities remain within the boundaries of the strategic domain of the firm. "Strategic context" processes refer to strategic domain definition and redefinition: the latter takes place when "middle managers" encourage "corporate management" to question the current strategy, helping them acknowledge and rationalise, ex post, the initiatives of successful "venture leaders".

In Burgelman's model, "venture leaders" are very much implied in the definition and impetus processes. They are backed by "middle managers" who, in their quality of organisational champions, help them get resources and top management support. At the top of the ladder, corporate managers monitor alignment and progress ("structural context") but sometimes have to modify their strategy in response to middle managers' suggestions ("strategic context").

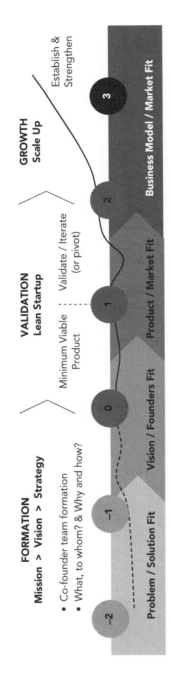

FORMATION
Mission > Vision > Strategy

- Co-founder team formation
- What, to whom? & Why and how?

VALIDATION
Lean Startup
Validate / Iterate (or pivot)

Minimum Viable Product

GROWTH
Scale Up

Establish & Strengthen

| Problem / Solution Fit | Vision / Founders Fit | Product / Market Fit | Business Model / Market Fit |

Ideating

Entrepreneurial ambition and/or potential scalable product or service idea for a big enough target market. Initial idea on how it would create value. One person or a vague team; no confirmed commitment or no right balance of skills in the team structure yet.

Concepting

Defining mission and vision with initial strategy and key milestones for next few years on how to get there. Two or three entrepreneurial core co-founders with complementary skills and ownership plan. Maybe additional team members for specific roles also with ownership.

Committing

Committed, skills balanced co-founding team with shared vision, values and attitude. Able to develop the initial product or service version, with committed resources, or already have initial product or service in place. Co-founders shareholder agreement (SHA) signed, including milestones, with shareholders time & money commitments, for next three years with proper vesting terms.

Validating

Iterating and testing assumptions for validated solution to demonstrate initial user growth and/or revenue. Initial Key Performance Indicators (KPI's) identified. Can start to attract additional resources (money or equity) via investments or loans for equity, interest or revenue share from future revenues.

Scaling

Focus on KPI based measurable growth in users, customers and revenues and/or market traction & market share in a big or fast growing target market. Can and want to grow fast. Consider or have attracted significant funding or would be able to do so if wanted. Hiring, improving quality and implementing processes.

Establishing

Achieved great growth, that can be expected to continue. Easily attract financial and people resources. Depending on vision, mission and commitments, will continue to grow and often tries to culturally continue "like a startup". Founders and/or investors make exit(s) or continue with the company.

Startup Development Phases - From idea to business and team to organization.

Version 3.0 - www.startupcommons.org

Figure 4.3 Start-up development phases (2016)

Source: www.startupcommons.org (2016).

Levels	Core Processes		Overlaying Processes	
	Definition	Impetus	Strategic Context	Structural Context
Top Management	Monitoring	Authorizing	Rationalizing _Selecting_	Structuring
Middle Management	Coaching Stewardship	_Product Championing_ Strategic Building	Delineating	Negotiating
Project Leader (Corporate Entrepreneur)	Technical and Need Linking	Strategic forcing	Gatekeeping Idea Generating Bootlegging	Questioning

Organizational Championing

Figure 4.4 Burgelman's process model of Internal Corporate Venturing

Source: Adapted from Burgelman (1983ASQ).

Burgelman's model posits a clear specialisation of tasks. Venture leaders are on the front line and can focus on creating and growing their business because they are backed by middle managers that deal with "political issues". Top managers act as "referees".

Venkataraman, McGrath and MacMillan's model (1992) also posits a clear specialisation of tasks. Here, each stage of the corporate venturing process has two facets: a techno-economical facet and a political one. "Corporate venturers" are in charge of economic and technological challenges, while "champions", that is, "powerful agents", take care of the political challenges. The economic/technological challenges evolve from "Ideating", to "Forcing", "Rollercoasting" and "Revitalising" (see Figure 4.5). These four challenges correspond to the NVD stages. The original contribution of Venkataraman et al. lies in their emphasis of "championing" as an integral part of Corporate Venturing. As the authors state: "internal championing is a necessary means by which the social and political pressures imposed by an existing organisation on a new venture are overcome or converted to the venture's advantage".

Championing initiates with "Idea Championing", a phase in which "powerful agents galvanize internal support for the business concept". It is followed by "Championing Opportunistic Behavior", a phase in which powerful agents "provide the authority to venture managers to break or modify existing routines (rules) if so warranted". In the "Resource Championing" stage, powerful agents put pressure on "resource allocators" to ensure that "sufficient resources are released for (its) development". In the final championing stage, "Championing Incorporation", powerful agents ensure that the new entity gets culturally and symbolically integrated in the organisation.

Economical/technological challenges:

Political challenges:

Figure 4.5 Venkataraman, McGrath and MacMillan's (1992) process model of Corporate Venturing

Source: Adapted from Venkataraman, McGrath and MacMillan (1992).

Figure 4.6 Our process model of Corporate Entrepreneurship

Our Corporate Entrepreneurship process model

Like Venkataraman et al.'s, our model views Corporate Entrepreneurship as a dual process in which both "market" and "political" challenges need to be addressed. However, instead of separating the two types of challenges, it blends them into a single sequence of five steps that correspond to the five key challenges that corporate entrepreneurs have to face as they go ahead with their venture (see Figure 4.6). Our model is evidence-based and combines observations performed on a large number of first-hand and second-hand corporate entrepreneurship case studies (cf. Appendix 1).

We will now review these five stages in detail.

Stage 1: Detect an opportunity

The journey of corporate entrepreneurs, like that of regular entrepreneurs, starts with the detection of an opportunity.[2] In the case of corporate entrepreneurs, however, this opportunity is not limited to a business idea: as Shane and Venkataraman (2000) underline, it could be any idea likely to improve corporate performance at large, measured in terms of competitive advantage, reputation in the community, internal climate, productivity, time to market and so on.

Technological innovation is a significant source of opportunity because it can help tackle previously insoluble problems, address unmet needs or better satisfy already targeted needs. It increases both the strategic and operational options of companies. The weaknesses of competitors are also an excellent source of opportunity: when competitors put in place abnormally high prices, when they offer poor service or neglect quality and innovation, they provide opportunities for their competitors. More generally, any change, whether it concerns the price and availability of raw materials, the distribution of wealth, lifestyle or social relations can be an opportunity. Population ageing, a major social and economic challenge in the next few decades, can be viewed as an opportunity as it generates a myriad of new, unsatisfied needs. This is also true of economic crises that reveal the obsolescence and inadequacy of prevalent business models.

Opportunity detection can be stimulated thanks to the use of creativity techniques. Indeed, opportunities often lie at the unexplored intersection of market/needs, on one hand, and product/technology on the other: employees looking for opportunities should systematically try to combine these two dimensions and explore what they could mean in practice. Frequently, the detection of opportunities results from the spontaneous association of previously unrelated activities or cognitive fields: Ian Telford, a corporate entrepreneur at Dow Chemical, imagined his innovative online chemicals selling site just after participating in a development seminar held in Silicon Valley (Chakravarthy and Huber, 2003). Joline Godfrey, of Polaroid Corp., imagined a new leisure activity using Polaroid cameras and films during her Mexican vacations (Hill, Kamprath and Conrad, 1992).

What looks like a nice idea on paper can be a dead end because of very basic issues such as limited market potential, technical limitations, excessive production costs and so on. It is therefore essential to test venture ideas as soon as possible. The engineer who is sure to hold the invention of the century should quickly contact a salesperson or a potential user; the salesperson certain to have identified a promising customer segment should check with production and logistics whether it can be served profitably. It is not pleasant to hear that one's brilliant idea does not hold water but there are advantages to hear negative comments early on: it allows corporate entrepreneurs to disengage quickly from a project that is not worth the trouble or, on the contrary, to reformulate and improve their initial concept.

The economic assessment of opportunities has to be performed several times throughout the venturing process. It is good practice to undertake this exercise as soon as possible: even though the projected revenues and costs appear quite uncertain at this stage, the efforts done to appraise them will help corporate entrepreneurs get a rough idea of the venture's breakeven point and help them identify its weaknesses. What matters at this stage are the orders of magnitude involved: are we talking about a small, large or medium project at company scale? Is it a project that requires significant investment but is potentially very profitable or a modest project with limited risks? This information will help the various stakeholders (corporate entrepreneurs included) understand the kind of project they are dealing with and take an initial stance. It will also provide indications as to who are the key stakeholders and most appropriate sponsors, as well as what performance metrics should be used to demonstrate the value of the project.

Corporate entrepreneurs are part of an organisation that faces unique challenges and pursues specific strategic objectives. It is in relation to these factors, not in absolute terms, that new opportunities should ultimately be assessed. Corporate entrepreneurs need a clear vision of the strengths and weaknesses of their company, its strategic direction and the short- and medium-term challenges it faces. Proper understanding of these elements will channel the creativity of corporate entrepreneurs in the right direction and thereby facilitate the identification of well-aligned opportunities.

Where there exist resources and processes allocated to Corporate Entrepreneurship, corporate entrepreneurs should contact those in charge and try and "sell" their idea as soon as possible. In this way, they will obtain early feedback and know their chances of getting support from the organisation. Corporate entrepreneurs should also try to identify which other projects are receiving support and why. This will help them position their own project.

Stage 2: Get initial support

Getting initial support is the first manifestation of the individual/organisation association we described in Chapter 2 (cf. Table 2.2) and that forms the backbone of successful Corporate Entrepreneurship. How and when initial support from a "powerful agent" should be sought depends on the level of autonomy of the corporate entrepreneur and their ability to mobilise informal resources within and outside the company. It also depends on the complexity and size of the project. Sooner or later, however, all corporate entrepreneurs are confronted by the limits of an autonomous approach and need to find a sponsor. A sponsor can be defined as follows:

> A senior management role that typically involves approving or supporting the allocation of resources for a venture, defining its goals and assessing the venture's eventual success. Furthermore, a project sponsor might also champion or advocate for the project to be adopted with other members of senior management within the business.
>
> (Business Dictionary)[3]

Should corporate entrepreneurs formalise their status and project as soon as possible or, conversely, should they keep a low profile as long as possible? The answer to this question depends on the nature of the project, the individuals involved and the context. In companies where politics count more than results, the explicit support of at least one influential leader is usually a condition for survival. If corporate entrepreneurs have access to resources and if, moreover, their idea has little chance of instantly seducing the senior managers of the company, then a strategy of "fait accompli" may prove effective: the satisfaction of the first customers and the enthusiasm of colleagues will be the best arguments to convince senior management of the value of their project. This approach, however, is risky and should be carefully evaluated before being adopted. Generally speaking, the more corporate entrepreneurs wait to formalise their project, the more the project runs the risk of being perceived as "Not Invented Here". On the other hand, the longer they remain invisible, the more time they have to perfect their concept and prove its value.

Getting initial support from a "powerful agent" is easier when:

(1) The corporate entrepreneur(s) is(are) known and appreciated by several members of the organisation.
(2) The project looks economically attractive and it is aligned with the strategic objectives of the organisation.
(3) The company's context and culture are favourable to Corporate Entrepreneurship.

To increase the attractiveness of their project, corporate entrepreneurs need to identify and then manage the **key stakeholders**. Stakeholders are many, diverse and often pursue contradictory goals. Some stakeholders have

---

Box 4.1 The company's context is not favourable to corporate entrepreneurs when...

- Innovation is viewed as the exclusive prerogative of marketing and R&D
- Top management is strongly focused on cash flow maximisation (in the context of a leveraged buy-out for example)
- Top management is exclusively focused on short-term (quarterly) results
- The organisation is organised in "silos" that hardly communicate
- There are no funds earmarked to support employee initiatives
- There are no formal procedures to assess employee initiatives
- The organisation is process oriented and responsibilities are diluted
- Failure and risk-taking are stigmatised

---

more weight than others and their perception of the project's attractiveness will be decisive. Corporate entrepreneurs must dedicate time and effort to identify who are the key stakeholders, understand their agenda and perceptions and engage in individual conversations. Corporate entrepreneurs must regularly probe their immediate and less immediate environment: they must check whether their project interferes with the plans of a colleague, whether it disturbs another department for unknown reasons and ensure they do not make enemies ready to evoke any pretext to block the project. They must understand what lies behind a declared or hidden hostility, find a compromise or, even better, devise a creative solution that satisfies everyone.

Lack of experience, poor knowledge of key stakeholders and their interests, a partial view of the organisation and its processes and an underdeveloped personal network are major blocks on the path to success. To compensate for these shortcomings, corporate entrepreneurs must secure the advice and protection of sympathetic and influential managers who will guide them, help them find resources and act as champions for their project.

Stage 3: Get official support

Thanks to the initial support they obtained, corporate entrepreneurs are able to prepare themselves for their next challenge: obtaining the official support of their company's senior management. In order to get official support, corporate

---

Box 4.2 The ideal sponsor

A candid self-diagnosis is definitely the best way to initiate the search for a sponsor. Does the corporate entrepreneur lack visibility? A high-profile manager, eager to shine by being associated with a promising and original project will be indicated. Is the corporate entrepreneur young and lacking political savviness? A fatherly figure who can also act as a mentor would be appropriate. Is the corporate entrepreneur experienced and technically proficient but weak in marketing and sales? A successful developer would be their best ally.

Sometimes, the direct superior of the corporate entrepreneur can be an appropriate sponsor. If this person is open to the initiatives of their employees and has a good reputation in the organisation, they could be a good sponsor. But the attitude of a direct superior could suddenly shift if they are put under pressure: the superior might stop supporting the corporate entrepreneur and require them to get back to basics and focus on regular tasks.

Over time, the needs of corporate entrepreneurs change and so will the "added value" of their sponsors. Corporate entrepreneurs should therefore consider changing sponsors as their project and its stakes evolve.

---

entrepreneurs need to prove both the viability of their project and their ability to develop it. In practice, this implies:

*   A growing engagement on the part of corporate entrepreneurs who must now work hard on their project while, in many cases, continuing to carry out their regular duties
*   Creating and managing a team of contributors
*   Optimising the use of limited financial resources
*   Overcoming mounting organisational resistance
*   Last, but not least, developing a working prototype or pilot of their idea

Let us now review the key success factors of this Corporate Entrepreneurship stage. Considering the interests of the main stakeholders is undoubtedly the first key success factor of this stage and one that cannot be overlooked. Indeed, the challenge is not only to "sell" the project internally by showing it in a good light, but also to integrate the requirements of key stakeholders in the project design, be they customers, suppliers or company managers whose activities are potentially impacting or impacted. This will help neutralise opposition and ensure the active collaboration of key stakeholders.

At this stage of the process, corporate entrepreneurs need to test the viability of their concept by elaborating convincing prototypes and conducting successful pilot experiments. There are usually trade-offs to be made between the degree of perfection of prototypes on the one hand and costs and deadlines on the other. Sometimes, it may be wise to settle for a less than perfect prototype that can be quickly shared and tested. In other cases, even a minor technical imperfection could disqualify the budding project.

According to the ambition and complexity of the venture project, developing a working prototype can be relatively straightforward or, on the contrary, it could require significant commitment and resources. At this stage of the corporate venturing process, there is usually a significant gap between the resources needed and the resources available to corporate entrepreneurs. This gap is usually filled thanks to the "free" help and contribution of colleagues, internal and external experts, suppliers and so on, which imply strong personal connections, both inside and outside the company.

In parallel to prototyping and testing, corporate entrepreneurs need to elaborate a thorough and convincing business plan. As this is a key success factor, corporate entrepreneurs need to be good at it or get the help of expert colleagues. A business plan has different functions and all are important:

- A business plan allows corporate entrepreneurs to clarify, test and improve their concept
- A business plan helps convince decision makers to invest in the project
- A business plan constitutes a blueprint for the implementation phase and provides a reference framework for the future decisions and actions of corporate entrepreneurs

Corporate entrepreneurs often compete with other organisational members when it comes to getting managerial attention and resources. To successfully promote their project, they need to study internal competition: they need to know what other projects are presently vying for resources, how attractive and high priority they are, who supports or opposes them and whether they are similar or potentially complementary with their own project.

Once they have elaborated a convincing prototype, shown the economic attractiveness of their venture project and properly positioned it within the company's new project portfolio, corporate entrepreneurs are ready to defend it in front of the official approval body of their company. This is the occasion, for senior managers, to meet with the whole project team and assess its degree of cohesion and commitment. It is important therefore to make sure that not only the project and the project leader are perceived positively but that the team, as a whole, is viewed as a major asset.

Stage 4: Make it happen (the implementation stage)

Once their venture project has obtained the official backing of senior managers, corporate entrepreneurs have greater legitimacy within the organisation and can more easily access the resources needed to turn their project into a reality. Their challenge is now to scale up their project and create/manage the organisation that will allow them to do so. Compared with the previous stages which mostly required creativity, flexibility communication and political skills, this new stage demands a great deal of determination on the part of corporate entrepreneurs, as well as substantial operational and managerial skills.

The implementation stage marks a turning point in the course of the Corporate Entrepreneurship process. Both the corporate entrepreneur and the organisation have to substantially increase their level of commitment and risk-taking. The corporate entrepreneur, who until now had kept some room for manoeuvre, may now have to leave his former job and be exposed to the gaze and criticism of his colleagues. Senior managers are investing money and reputation on a highly visible project. For both parties, the possibility of failure is now heavy with consequences.

Depending on the size and complexity of the project, this stage often marks the transition from a solo configuration to a team configuration. The priorities of corporate entrepreneurs evolve: designing and communicating become less important activities, deploying resources, leading a team, meeting deadlines and achieving results are the new challenges. Project management and team management skills become critical. Corporate entrepreneurs must create and strengthen their team, set tasks and motivate. But success does not only depend on team performance. It generally requires the cooperation of a multitude of internal stakeholders (IT, legal services, manufacturing, sales, etc.). Getting this cooperation is a challenge, which requires the crafty use of both stick and carrot. Corporate entrepreneurs have to win sympathy, respect and consent, combining relational skills and negotiators' talent and reminding their colleagues, from time to time, that their endeavour has powerful backers.

The implementation phase is the moment of truth for the project. The transition from a small-scale to a full-size project is indeed a considerable challenge. All kinds of difficulties may arise at this stage: a prospective supplier is not reliable, there are unforeseen technical issues, costs are higher than estimated, a competitor is about to launch a similar offer and so on. Despite these unexpected challenges, economic goals must be met and, to this end, an efficient value chain has to be put in place. Even at this stage, because of unforeseen events or wrong assumptions, pivotal changes – changing the business model from B to C to B to B, performing internally an activity that should have been outsourced and so on – might be required. Unforeseen changes combined with time constraints sometimes demand calculated risk-taking on the part of corporate entrepreneurs, raising the question of what is an acceptable level of risk for the organisation and how much risk they can take, given their fuzzy employee-entrepreneur status.

Stage 5: Plan the exit

When corporate entrepreneurs engage in a new project, they rarely contemplate what will happen once it is completed. There are nonetheless very different potential end-stage scenarios: corporate entrepreneurs could continue managing the activity they have created or they could hand it in to someone else and get involved in a new, challenging project. They could go back to their previous job or want to change job. To make the most out of the venture, corporate entrepreneurs need to imagine various exit scenarios and discuss them with their sponsors and managers. They should also clarify and share their expectations in terms of rewards in case of success. Here again, there are many possible scenarios (see Box 4.3).

In summary

☐ Research shows that Corporate Entrepreneurship is a dual process: it combines a **venturing process** in which a business idea is progressively transformed from a concept – a prototype – to an activity that gets progressively scaled up into an established business AND an **organisational process** by which the venture progressively gains legitimacy, obtains resources internally and establishes structural and strategic ties with the rest of the organisation.

☐ Several organisational actors are implied in the Corporate Entrepreneurship process. Apart from the corporate entrepreneur himself, "powerful agents" intervene as champions and sponsors in favour of the corporate entrepreneurs' projects. Senior management provides strategic

---

Box 4.3 Rewarding corporate entrepreneurs

The motivation of entrepreneurs depends on several factors: intrinsic factors – building a new business is in itself very exciting – and extrinsic ones, such as the prospect of acquiring wealth, autonomy and prestige. In their effort to foster entrepreneurial behaviours, organisations rely heavily on the inherent appeal of developing a project from A to Z, testing oneself and being able to "make a difference" with which they combine extrinsic rewards defined *ex ante* and common to all corporate entrepreneurs or negotiated *ex post* with each individual. The most common extrinsic rewards are:

– Money (prize, bonus, percentage of the value created, options to buy shares of future venture)
– Recognition and visibility within the company
– Letting the corporate entrepreneurs choose their next move: manage the activity, move to a new venture, take a break, get promoted and so on

---

orientations, adapts them, manages the overall innovation portfolio and rewards successful corporate entrepreneurs.

☐ Corporate entrepreneurs face five major challenges as they go along: (1) they must identify a valid opportunity; (2) they must get initial support from a "powerful agent" inside the company; (3) they must gain the official support of the company's top management; (4) they must "make the project happen"; and (5) they must plan the exit.

☐ Each stage of the Corporate Entrepreneurship process has specific key success factors (see Table 4.1) and requires different skills and competencies on the part of corporate entrepreneurs.

To go further

Study questions:

1. Can any employee with a good project succeed as a corporate entrepreneur? Justify your answer.

Table 4.1 The five challenges of corporate entrepreneurs: key success factors

Detect an opportunity	Get initial support	Get official support	Make it happen	Plan the exit
(1) An open and curious mind	(1) A generally favourable organisational context	(1) Taking key stakeholders' interests into account	(1) Being committed and persistent	(1) Anticipating
(2) Access to original information about customers, competition, technologies and trends	(2) An attractive project that is aligned with the strategic objectives of the company	(2) Developing a working prototype	(2) Creating and motivating a multi-disciplinary team	(2) Clarifying expectations
(3) Knowledge of strategic issues facing the company, business unit and department	(3) Being a known and appreciated employee	(3) Writing a convincing business plan (4) Constantly promoting the project	(3) Establishing productive links with various part of the organisation	
			(4) Constantly adapting and taking calculated risks	

2.   What can companies do to help corporate entrepreneurs face their five key challenges? What can managers do to help employees detect relevant opportunities? What can they do to help them find initial support? How can they help them get the official support of senior managers? How can they facilitate the implementation phase and, finally, the exit phase?
3.   Which stage is the most risky and/or complex? Why?
4.   Go back to any of the mini-cases presented in the previous chapters and try to identify the challenges of corporate entrepreneurs and the Corporate Entrepreneurship process stages in the narrative.

Notes

1 Section 4.2 draws partly on the literature review in Backholm (1999).
2 Opportunity: "Exploitable set of circumstances with uncertain outcome, requiring commitment of resources and involving exposure to risk" (www.businessdictionary.com/definition/opportunity.html#ixzz4CnLbE5dn; Accessed 2 August 2017).
3 www.businessdictionary.com/definition/project-sponsor.html#ixzz4D94cKAN8 (Accessed 2 August 2017).

Team dynamics and management in Corporate Entrepreneurship

5

In the previous chapter, we saw that Corporate Entrepreneurship was a dual process in which both "market" (external) and "political" (organisational) challenges need to be addressed. Corporate entrepreneurs constantly interact with other members of the organisation and success depends on their ability to manage relationships with key actors, adapting them as their project moves through various stages.

Corporate Entrepreneurs are often **members of teams**, especially in the later stages of their project, and as such, also face the challenge of making their team work smoothly and effectively. In this chapter, we will look at how entrepreneurial teams should be constituted and managed, combining the latest research on entrepreneurial teams with the results of our own case study analyses.[1]

We will focus on two key factors for success in the creation and management of entrepreneurial teams: (1) the existence of complementarities within the team and (2) the team's ability to develop collective skills.

Complementarity of skills, individual profiles and networks

Complementarity of skills

Sooner or later, entrepreneurial teams find themselves needing to cover the company's key operational fields: research and development, production, marketing and sales, finance and management. The difficulty can be in how to allocate these different functions, the general rule being to give the responsibilities of an operational field to someone who has concrete experience in it. When it does not correspond to the demands of a project or company, it is therefore preferable to avoid mono-cultural and mono-skilled groups. A diversity of educational pathways and professional experiences offers a wide range of skills to be drawn upon, all the better to enable a variety of responses when faced with the heterogeneity of situations to come.

An analysis of complementarities in terms of skills must stem from the needs and demands of the project and the future company. What are the most essential and useful skills? This question, once asked, will serve as a reference point allowing each member to try and specify, as faithfully as possible, the following points:

(1) main skills gained through education (compulsory and further education);
(2) main professional responsibilities;
(3) sectors and activities in which these responsibilities have been exercised;
(4) skills and knowledge confirmed by experience;
(5) main professional successes;
(6) main professional strengths; and
(7) main professional limitations.

This kind of approach is the basis of team building: knowing oneself and sharing knowledge in all fields covered by the team in order to be able to identify duplication and shortcomings and to allow every team member to find their place. By working this way, it is possible to identify fields that are not covered which correspond to the key factors of success. In such cases, the project needs to be realigned or a regular long-term staff member or partner should be found.

Complementarity of personalities and aptitudes

What is needed is a balance of temperaments amongst the different team members: they need to bring together the go-getter, the deep thinker, the optimist, the prudent, the creative innovator and the rigorous organiser in order to create a strong collective. It goes without saying that a team with one person who is imaginative and able to identify (or construct) opportunities and another who can translate these ideas in economic terms through organisational ability is stronger than a team with only one of these aptitudes. As with skills, the analysis of complementarities in terms of personalities and aptitudes should be carried out openly, first at an individual level, and then collectively.

But combining complementarities is not always enough. A team can include two members who complement one another in terms of skills and personalities, but who cannot agree on priorities in terms of target growth, risk-taking and organisation. This can be the case, for example, with groups containing members who favour permanence and independence and for whom one of the main concerns is to ensure the venture's survival – making them risk-averse – and corporate entrepreneurs who seek growth, for whom the main objective involves a higher level of risk.

Complementarity of networks

An association of individuals can also bring together complementary relationship networks. Indeed, very often, members who have followed different pathways find complementarity in personal and professional networks. This is an important point that should not be neglected.

A growing number of research studies show that whilst diversity within a team is a source of strength and skill, the consequence can be conflict, which must be managed. Even more than diversity, though, what counts is the team's ability to get on and be collectively competent.

Collective competence

Collective competence is the key to taking advantage of **complementarities** $(1 + 1 = 3)$. The notion of collective competence can be defined as, "The entire know-how that comes from a working team, combining the endogenous and exogenous resources of each of its members and creating new competencies from a synergistic combination of resources" (Amherdt et al., 2000, cited by Naffakhi, 2011, p. 13). In the entrepreneurial context, where this concept starts to be explored, four key conditions emerge:

(1)   Knowing how to learn together from past experience
(2)   Drawing on common motivations and values
(3)   Creating confidence within the team
(4)   Agreeing on leadership and taking decisions accepted by all

Knowing how to learn together from past experience

The first condition consists in knowing how to learn lessons from the results of each action. The survey conducted by Naffakhi in 2011 on team members of seven companies shows the centrality of the collective learning process for optimal decision-making. They describe this process as a cycle of rapid and uncertain decisions in a trial/error mode leading to better or worse consequences that requires distance and perspective to make better decisions in the future. A particularly important point is to accept failure as a learning opportunity and not as a dead end (Naffakhi, 2011).

The second course of learning cited by the team members of this survey is mutual learning by observation of the reactions and reasoning of other group members. This confirms one of the theoretical ideas of Shepherd and Krueger (2002) on the collective cognition of entrepreneurial teams; that is, a vicarious learning process or modelling between members of the team. The fact that team members do not have the same perception and interpretation in relation to a problem but that they have chosen to respond to it together helps create a fruitful confrontation of viewpoints. The benefit is a more open mindset from the members and the ability to interpret signals from the wider environment as well as to better mobilise exterior resources. A verbatim extract cited in this research clearly explains the learning process in place.

> I think that what I learned from X, is a very open mind. In fact, X is someone whose mind is constantly working and actually unfailingly open about everything. I mean, (this person) is like a sponge and so I learned that, I learned to use that sponge, actually, and to try to be like that sponge.
>
> (Naffakhi, 2011, p. 23)

For confrontation to be beneficial, the distances between the different points of view must not be too great in cognitive terms. West (2007) showed in a longitudinal study on management teams of 22 technology start-ups in the development phase that their points of view on the strategic factors should have moderate degrees of differentiation (divergence of analysis on a given factor) and integration (agreement on the relative pertinence of factors to be considered) in order to have a positive impact on venture performance. The keys for interpreting points of view regarding actions must also be shared, namely, the motivations of team members to act on a project should be more or less convergent.

Drawing on convergent values and motivations with regard to venture creation

Shepherd and Krueger (2002) offer a theoretical model of collective cognition for entrepreneurial teams. In order to reach shared agreements, they suggest that the different points of view and information used by the members of the team should be able to be interpreted in terms of convergent desirability and feasibility. Several subjects of agreement are presented as being decisive for favouring the emergence of shared understanding regarding environment and decisions to be taken for the company:

- Shared values on the importance of failures as learning opportunities
- A shared attitude regarding risks and innovation
- Agreement on the objectives for growth and autonomy of the venture and on acceptable level of risk
- Shared beliefs about the benefit of seeking new clients

We believe that establishing a dialogue from the start on the relationship of each team member with regard to risk and autonomy is essential in order to later decide together about desired growth and an exit strategy. Thus, from the first stages of the project, the team members have everything to gain from considering themselves as being in experimental situations that can allow them to get to grips with their future responsibilities. This gives them a chance to check that they are comfortable in their roles, given the context and environment. This learning process can reveal the different personalities and motivations working towards becoming members of the venture. Working in this way, over a certain period and with high regularity (several months and a number of working meetings) constitutes a very good way of validating certain fundamental elements of the team. Generally, during this process, many things will be clarified as evidence, while confirmations and doubts appear. It would be preferable to envisage changes within the team (exclusions, new members, modifications to the allocation or roles) from this stage onwards, whilst the cost of changes, including the psychological cost, remains reasonable. The least doubt, the slightest uncertainty in relation to oneself or others should be talked about. Waiting is very often a poor idea. The many cases we have observed through our teaching work compels us to insist very much on the need to sort out the problems and get rid of all the doubts within a team before really getting the project off the ground.

Creating trust and reciprocal obligations

Several recent studies use empirical evidence to underline the importance of cohesion in the entrepreneurial team as a factor supporting reflexivity and innovation, as well as increased trust. As the psychologist Mucchielli (2002, p. 46) states, trust is an essential ingredient in enabling groups made up of individuals with complementary competencies to be effective and innovative. Blatt (2009) explains that trust within a team involves accepting to show one's vulnerability in relation to others, but with the expectation that others will not exploit that vulnerability. This attitude allows more information to be exchanged and more divergent points of view to be confronted and thus to take decisions based on a wider pool of information. In addition, trust puts in place a virtuous circle of reciprocal obligations: if members trust others, they agree to delegate more tasks to them and feel more committed to giving the best of themselves to achieve their objectives. Finally, the members of the team feel that they belong to a collective they can identify with and which contributes to the construction of their social roles. It is therefore particularly important in order to learn together and feel united in action.

But, paradoxically, trust is not natural in entrepreneurial teams characterised by newness: it is, in fact, more difficult to build than in classical business teams. Generally, trust is built over time through accumulated shared experience, that is, through the construction of strong ties. We know that it is rarely the only source of recruitment in entrepreneurial teams and even when it is used in this way, previous strong ties are not necessarily relevant in the new venture context. What is more, the newness of the situation can have rather damaging consequences relating to the creation of trust. Indeed, uncertainty generates very strong but ambivalent feelings of excitement and stress that are different and of variable intensity according to each person. This obliges each person to invest more energy in understanding situations. When people build a new team together, each person's reactions can be unpredictable and sometimes difficult to understand and accept. In addition, taking on a new market does not favour the identification of shared and legitimate responses that might instil trust in the team. The degree of uncertainty of the situation puts everyone in undetermined roles, which leads to ambiguity regarding responsibilities, priorities and expected behaviour.

The members of the entrepreneurial team must therefore voluntarily adopt specific behaviour to make up for the negative effects of novelty on trust and mutual obligations. Blatt (2009) suggests two complementary ways of doing so:

(1) The adoption of principles of allocation of resources and shared advantage. The community principles suggest allocating resources on the basis of perceived needs and personal commitment. This allows members to better understand and accept the motivations and behavioural tendencies of other members, and therefore to better anticipate and respond to others' actions and for each member to be more committed because they feel that their efforts are being rewarded.

(2) Contractualisation; that is, the explanation of reciprocal expectations, notably in terms of tasks and responsibilities, and results in particular situations experienced together. Contractualisation, whether oral or in writing, is likely to create more trust between members. It can also encourage the emergence of responses recognised as useful, which can serve as models to be reproduced in another situation and/or by another member. Finally, it helps to make every member feel responsible and committed.

The two suggested approaches are complementary and inseparable because each taken on its own would have negative effects for the other. Contractualising responsibilities without recognising needs and commitment can become very formal and have no influence on behaviour. Recognising needs and commitment without specifying the responsibilities can push people in the wrong direction.

Agreeing on leadership and taking decisions accepted by all

Leadership can be defined in a simple way as the "ability to direct a group of individuals towards the accomplishment of precise goals and to mobilise them in the long-term" (Robbins, Judge, & Gabilliet, 2006, p. 412). Recent entrepreneurship research shows the benefits of the leader of an entrepreneurial team adopting an "open style, that shares communication, a critical ability and persuasion" (Naffakhi, 2011, p. 24) in order to encourage the emergence of the collective competence necessary for the team to learn from past experiences together. According to other studies, the leader of the entrepreneurial team should adopt a flexible style, knowing how to vary the degree of self-assertiveness and receptivity to others, according to the stress level of a situation and the needs of members. Other authors suggest that transformational leadership (focus on relationships) is better than transactional leadership (focus on tasks) for transmitting the entrepreneurship mindset within a team. Another research thread places the emphasis on the importance of authentic leadership based on ethical behaviour built on coherent values between words and actions and perceived as such by subordinates. In sharing information, encouraging subordinates to freely express whatever they wish whilst respecting their ideas, the authentic leader inspires and creates trust in the team.

Beyond leadership style, based on specific attitudes and communication strategies, we believe that it is useful in an entrepreneurial context to examine the leadership functions exercised by different members of a group. In fact, recent research on organisation highlights the idea that leadership is not always centred on one person, but can be distributed amongst different people. This is the case in autonomous teamwork settings where the tasks are particularly complex. The complexity makes it improbable that a single individual has the ability to successfully assume all leadership functions for the whole lifespan of the team. A leader can emerge in implicit terms in the same way that roles can be negotiated and shared between different group members. In this case, leadership consists of a "collection of roles and behaviour types that can be distributed, shared, moved and in a sequential or simultaneous way" (Barry, 1991, p. 34). Being emergent and relational in nature, shared leadership can lead to team members having mutual influence on one another and to even better performance than with centralised leadership.

The four functions of leadership identified by Barry (1991) – (1) envisioning leadership that elaborates a shared vision; (2) organising leadership that plans, shares and controls the carrying out of tasks; (3) spanning leadership that represents the team to the outside world; and (4) social leadership that encourages dialogue between members – could therefore be shared between the different team members.

When entrepreneurial teams are in the process of setting up, two functions appear crucial in order for the project to pass from the unknown to being recognised as feasible: the visionary function and the function of representing the group to the outside world. However, it is not certain that these two functions will have to be carried out by the same person, given that different members often share networking roles and that the key know-how behind the vision of the project sometimes comes from complementarity of competencies (for example, combining engineering IT invention and marketing to find new applications). In addition, when the team gets larger (from three or four members up) and/or when the challenges of innovation requires knowing how to generate ideas together before sharing the project with clients, supporters, sponsors or potential suppliers, the leadership functions involving effective organisation of tasks and facilitating team relations are at least as important as spanning and vision-related functions.

In summary

☐   The success of entrepreneurial teams relies on two basic conditions: (1) the existence of complementarities within the team and (2) the team's ability to develop collective skills.

☐   When constituting teams, several types of complementarity have to be assessed: skills complementarity, personal profiles complementarity and networks complementarity are among the most valuable ones.

☐   Skills complementarity is essential to ensure that the various aspects of the venture's operations are adequately configured and managed. Complementarity in terms of personalities and aptitudes is also essential to the success of an entrepreneurial team: a good team brings together the go-getter, the deep thinker, the optimist, the prudent, the creative innovator and the rigorous organiser. Although less critical than skills complementarity, networks complementarity also contributes to the success of the entrepreneurial team by increasing the array of accessible expertise and resources.

☐   Studies show that whilst diversity within a team is a source of strength and skill, one consequence can be conflict, which must be managed. More than diversity, what counts is the team's ability to get on and to be collectively competent. The notion of collective competence can be defined as, "The entire know-how that comes from a working team, combining the endogenous and exogenous resources of each of its members and creating new competencies from a synergistic combination of resources" (Amherdt et al., 2000, cited by Naffakhi, 2011, p. 13).

☐   For collective competence to emerge and grow, team members have to: (1) know how to learn together from past experience; (2) draw on common motivations and values; (3) experience trust within the team; and (4) agree on leadership and take decisions accepted by all.

☐   Trust is essential for collective competence: trust allows team members to show their vulnerabilities, thus allowing more information to be exchanged. It also allows more effective sharing of tasks and responsibilities among team members and less need for continuous control and coordination.

☐   Trust is favoured for (1) sound and explicit principles of allocation of resources and shared advantage among team members and

(2) contractualisation, which is the explanation of reciprocal expectations, notably in terms of tasks and responsibilities, and results in particular situations experienced together.

☐ The complexity implied in successfully managing a corporate venture makes it improbable that a single individual has the ability to successfully assume all leadership functions for the whole lifespan of the team. Leadership will then consist of a "collection of roles and behaviour types that can be distributed, shared, moved . . . in a sequential or simultaneous way" (Barry, 1991, p. 34).

To go further

Go back to the mini-case, "The TV on ADSL Project" (Box 1.4) and analyse the challenges faced by Silvia throughout the main phases of the project. For each phase, propose an ideal team configuration, briefly describing each member's skills, network and personality.

Do you think that Silvia should maintain her leadership throughout the various phases of the project or should other team members take over as the challenges facing the team evolve?

Note

1 Part of this chapter is adapted from previous work by the authors (Fayolle, 2012).

Part 3

Implementing Corporate Entrepreneurship: learning from experience

In this last part, we look closely at how companies encourage Corporate Entrepreneurship in practice. Relying on our observation of actual Corporate Entrepreneurship implementation attempts, the final part includes:

- An identification of the set of "enablers" most commonly put in place to encourage and support Corporate Entrepreneurship initiatives and entrepreneurial behaviours (Chapter 6).
- A review the organisational devices put in place to induce Corporate Entrepreneurship (Chapter 7).
- A conclusion of the underlying design principles that are common to all Corporate Entrepreneurship implementation attempts, showing how they encourage but can also end up constraining employees' entrepreneurial initiatives and behaviours (Chapter 8).

Implementing Corporate Entrepreneurship: the key enablers   **6**

Introduction

Entrepreneurial behaviours within established firms imply a degree of employee autonomy that can make management problematic (Burgelman, 1984; Kanter, 1985; Kanter et al., 1990; Stevenson and Jarillo, 1990). Sathe (1985) believes that, for this reason, Corporate Entrepreneurship raises a fundamental dilemma and Thornberry (2001) goes as far as calling it an "oxymoron". This has not discouraged managers of large and small firms – for decades now – to try and encourage entrepreneurial behaviours, with a view to foster growth and innovation, accelerate development cycles, improve employee motivation and, ultimately, increase the firm's competitiveness.

As apparent in the comparative case studies of Kanter et al. (1990, 1991a, 1991b), Kanter, Quinn and North (1992), Stopford and Baden-Fuller (1994) and in Wolcott and Lippitz's (2007a) more recent typology, Corporate Entrepreneurship approaches to implementation vary greatly in terms of their **scope**. Some implementation attempts involve just a few individuals working on a single project, whereas others affect several hundred – in some cases, several thousand – employees, thus giving rise to a multitude of entrepreneurial initiatives. Scope, as we will see, has a major impact on organisational dynamics and outcomes, as well as on resources, the organisational and managerial tools that need to be deployed in order to foster Corporate Entrepreneurship.

The heterogeneity of implementation approaches is also a consequence of the wide array of goals that different firms pursue. Kanter et al. (1990) observe that the firms who put in place "entrepreneurial engines" pursue either economic or cultural goals and that this initial orientation has strong implications on the "engines" put in place, employee participation and management. Stopford and Baden-Fuller (1994) distinguish three stages of entrepreneurial development, corresponding to top management's growing level of commitment to Corporate Entrepreneurship. Different inducing structures and processes characterise each stage. Covin and Miles (1999) identify four forms of Corporate Entrepreneurship according to whether the aim is to renew products and markets, the organisation, the strategy or the domain of activity of the firm. Miles and Covin (2002) observe that Corporate Venture Units can be classified according to the focus of entrepreneurship – internal or external, while Hill and Birkinshaw (2008), according to their "strategic logic"; that is, the exploitation of existing opportunities or the exploration of new ones.

In order to reach their Corporate Entrepreneurship objectives, companies deploy organisational and managerial tools or "enablers", ranging from communication campaigns to project selection procedures, information systems to incentive schemes, training and coaching programmes to dedicated organisational entities and earmarked financial envelopes. In previous chapters, we have named these unique combinations of enablers aiming at encouraging and supporting Corporate Entrepreneurship, *Corporate Entrepreneurship Devices*. In this chapter, these enablers will be reviewed one by one.

The extant literature on Corporate Entrepreneurship "enablers" is substantial. Kuratko, Montagno and Hornsby (1990) mention, among the most important, (1) the level of commitment of top managers; (2) the organisational structure; and (3) the availability of resources and rewards. For Garvin (2002), the conditions of successful Corporate Venturing are (1) valuing risk taking; (2) resource availability (time and money); (3) a long-term perspective and *patient money*; and (4) the creation of dedicated organisational units.

Hayton (2005) identifies five HR practices that impact Corporate Entrepreneurship: (1) socialisation and team-building training; (2) job designs that favour employees' autonomy; (3) cross-functional team organisation; (4) incentives and performance evaluation that promotes risk-taking behaviours; and (5) perceived management support for entrepreneurial activities. Brazeal, Schenkel and Azriel (2008) mention (1) the motivation and support of top management; (2) the level of autonomy and freedom of employees; (3) time availability; (4) transparent and well communicated managerial expectations associated with formal mechanisms of evaluation, selection and diffusion of innovation; and (5) granting rewards. Morris et al. (2009) identify four elements needed to create a climate favourable to Intrapreneurship and underline the interdependence of (1) corporate culture; (2) firm structure; (3) formal and informal resource control mechanisms;

and (4) HR policies. They suggest that median positions between individualism and collectivism (corporate culture), autonomy and restriction (structure), easy and difficult access to resources (control mechanism), performance based rewards and job safety and administrative competencies and entrepreneurial competencies (HR policies), are the most favourable to Corporate Entrepreneurship.

These authors draw lists of "enablers" that differ slightly but that are, overall, coherent. They also suggest that, in spite of the great variety of Corporate Entrepreneurship implementation approaches, success depends on all the enablers to be present simultaneously. The careful analysis of our Corporate Entrepreneurship implementation cases has led us to take a different stance. We have observed that certain "enablers" were more diffuse than others and that they were combined according to recurrent patterns. By systematically analysing the cases at hand, we were able to identify seven key enablers and observed that, while some enablers were always mentioned (top management commitment, for example), others were less diffuse (see Table 6.1). We will now review each key enabler in detail.

Explicit commitment of the top management in favour of Corporate Entrepreneurship

Extant literature strongly emphasises the all-important role of top managers in encouraging Corporate Entrepreneurship. Top managers should be hands on (Herbert and Brazeal, 2004), convey a vision (Ireland, Covin and Kuratko, 2009) and provide unwavering moral and material support to corporate entrepreneurs (MacMillan, Block and Narasimha, 1986; Kuratko and Montagno, 1989; Morris and Jones, 1999; Garvin, 2002). Burgelman (1983ASQ), on the contrary, emphasises the crucial role played by middle managers in articulating the strategic requirements of internal new ventures with extant organisational capabilities and operational constraints. Wolcott and Lippitz (2007a) underline the positive role that well-connected corporate "veterans" can actually play.

As inducing Corporate Entrepreneurship at company level is first and foremost a senior managers' decision, an explicit commitment of the part of top management, not surprisingly, comes out as the most widespread "enabler" in our case base. Notwithstanding, we observed that top management commitment does vary considerably, both in nature and intensity. In companies such as L'Oréal, 3M, Google or W.L. Gore,[2] top management powerfully conveyed its approval of entrepreneurial behaviour and commitment to supporting

Table 6.1 Implementing Corporate Entrepreneurship: the key enablers and their occurrence[1]

Enabler	Modalities
Explicit commitment of top management in favour of Corporate Entrepreneurship Occ.: 27	Through statements and attitudes Occ.: 16 Through direct monitoring of performance Occ.: 15
Providing islands of autonomy in the workplace to foster Corporate Entrepreneurship Occ.: 26	Creating a separate entity Occ.: 11 Creating an operationally independent entity Occ.: 4 Providing an entrepreneurial pathway Occ.: 5 Maintaining a flat and decentralised structure Occ.: 7
Improving communication and access to information Occ.: 24	Organising events (seminars, workshops, fairs) and/or setting up IT enabled information and communication tools Occ.: 15 Working in small, close-knit team(s) Occ.: 19
Promoting Corporate Entrepreneurship through HR policies Occ.: 18	Hiring and/or staffing Occ.: 17 Training Occ.: 7
Setting up ad hoc incentive and reward systems Occ.: 16	Offering financial rewards Occ.: 7 Offering symbolic rewards Occ.: 11 Tying performance appraisal to entrepreneurial attitudes Occ.: 5
Establishing a formal entrepreneurial project evaluation and support process Occ.: 15	
Implementing an ad hoc time allocation policy Occ.: 5	Conditional time allocation Occ.: 2 Free time rule Occ.: 3

projects and rewarding corporate entrepreneurs. The launches of "Enter-Prize" (Ohio Bell), "Myriad Ideas" (Schneider Electric) and "IDClic" (Orange FT France) were supported by intense internal communication campaigns involving managers at the highest level.

Several Corporate Entrepreneurship implementation attempts in our case base were directly supervised or sponsored by companies' or divisions' top managers: it is the case for the "Change Agent Program" (Siemens Nixdorf), the "New Ventures Group" (Lucent Technologies), the "New Venture Organization" (Nokia) and for most single internal ventures surveyed (the "NEES Energy Venture", "Serengeti Eyewear", "Projet TV sur ADSL", "MEMS Unit", etc.).

We found that top management commitment expresses itself through (1) statements and attitudes, amplified and relayed through various means of communication and/or (2) the establishment of direct connections with corporate entrepreneurs. The first modality strongly impacts employees' representations, while the second directly affects their means of action. Indeed, reporting directly to top management implies frequent progress monitoring but also enhanced visibility and better access to resources.

Providing islands of autonomy in the workplace

The literature (Burgelman, 1983MS; Lumpkin and Dess, 1996; Bouchard and Bos, 2006; Lumpkin, Cogliser and Schneider, 2009) identifies autonomy as one, if not the defining component of Corporate Entrepreneurship. Autonomy takes various forms and can be observed at different levels. Brazeal, Schenkel and Azriel (2008) claim that employee autonomy is a basic requirement of Corporate Entrepreneurship, while several authors (Brazeal, 1993; Garvin, 2002; Herbert and Brazeal, 2004; Ireland, Covin and Kuratko, 2009; Morris et al., 2009) view the creation of autonomous organisational units as the most effective enabler of Corporate Entrepreneurship. Burgers et al. (2009) show that "structural differentiation", that is, organisational autonomy, does contribute to the effectiveness of corporate venturing. Autonomy can also take the form of earmarked funds available to corporate entrepreneurs, provided their project respects some pre-established criteria (Wolcott and Lippitz, 2007a). The issue of resource availability and the autonomy it provides is a recurrent theme when discussing the conditions for Corporate Entrepreneurship (Kuratko, Hornsby and Goldsby, 2004; Ireland, Covin and Kuratko, 2009). Some authors mention perceived availability of resources as a favourable factor (Kanter, 1985; Sathe, 1985; Sykes and Block, 1989). For Burgelman and Sayles (1986), the existence of "slack resources" encourages experimentation and risk-taking, and for Damanpour (1991), it determines organisational innovation. Other authors emphasise the importance of adequate funding (Von Hippel, 1977; Kuratko, Covin and Garrett, 2009) and "patient money"

(Garvin, 2002). Finally, Morris et al. (2009) advocate a "balanced resource control": corporate entrepreneurs should have access to, not too many, nor too few resources.

Unsurprisingly, "providing autonomy in the workplace" is the second most recurrent enabler in our case base. Yet one can observe that employee autonomy too often gets stifled by short-term operational priorities, tortuous decision processes and rigid corporate processes. This is why it is often necessary to create *protected areas* within which employees can enjoy greater autonomy and access the resources (money, expertise, sponsorship) needed to pursue innovative or divergent projects. Various solutions are put in place to this effect: the most radical one consists of creating a separate and autonomous entity, with its own resources and hierarchically independent from other operational divisions. This was, for example, the approach at P&G when the top management created the "Corporate New Ventures" division or at Lucent Technologies when it created the "New Ventures Division". Such entities define their own strategies, manage their project portfolio, operate with their own management structures, timeline and performance criteria and their staff can devote themselves entirely to the pursuit of innovative projects.

A slightly less radical solution consists in setting up a separate entity that is autonomous in its operations but not so when it comes to its strategy and project portfolio. Typically, these entities are monitored via joint steering committees and connected to the rest of the organisation via various communication channels (e.g. Raytheon's "NPC" or Nokia's "NVO"). Another less radical solution consists of developing entrepreneurial sponsorship and implementation pathways that enable employees who wish to develop projects to get the resources and support they need independently of their direct superior's approval, at least in the initial stages of their project. While on this entrepreneurial pathway, employees are guided, put in relationships with experts and potential sponsors, provided with seed money and encouraged to work on their project without abandoning their regular job. Such entrepreneurial pathways have been adopted at Ohio Bell ("Enter-Prize" programme), Kodak Eastman ("Offices of Innovation" and "New Opportunity Development"), Schneider Electric ("Mille Idées") and Orange FT France ("IDClic").

A fourth way to encourage autonomy and personal initiative is to maintain a high level of decentralisation and to favour flat organisational structures. To avoid "bureaucratisation", whenever an operational unit reaches a certain size, it is encouraged to split so as to preserve its manageability and responsiveness. This is the policy adopted by L'Oréal, W.L. Gore and 3M and it also appears to be a key feature of Acordia's and HomeServe's managerial philosophy.

Improving communication and access to information

With the exceptions of Simsek et al. (2009) and Castrogiovanni, Urbano and Loras (2011), who mention that enhanced communication and adequate information systems can play a role in encouraging Corporate Entrepreneurship, this enabler has not been emphasised in the literature. Yet, in a majority of the cases surveyed, enhanced communication and shared information played a significant role in facilitating Corporate Entrepreneurship.

Better communication between employees across units, functions and levels, better information flow between the upstream (technology experts) and the downstream of the value chain (market experts) and exposure to diverse realities (other industries, markets or strategies) significantly increase employees' perceptions of opportunities and foster new ideas for products, business models and internal processes. The head of P&G's "Corporate New Ventures" launched his new venture entity with an intensive creativity seminar and made sure his team had contacts with experts of all sorts and regularly participated in trade fairs. The leaders of "Enter-Prize" created annual internal fairs in which corporate entrepreneurs were able to showcase their projects, thus encouraging other employees to take initiatives. Similarly, "IDClic" participants are allowed to try and "sell" their project to Orange FT top managers at an "idea market" organised once a year.

Ad hoc information systems can also contribute to Corporate Entrepreneurship. In order to make the right decisions, employees need to be informed of the firm's strategic orientations and priorities. They must know about market, technological and competitive evolutions and, finally, they must know "who does what, and where". At Orange FT, all the proposed projects and their state of advancement are visible online to all employees, who can peruse them for inspiration and to improve their own projects. Orange FT and HomeServe also provide sophisticated electronic tools to help corporate entrepreneurs identify internal experts and best practices in a few clicks.

A simple and effective way to intensify communication and information exchange is to rely on small, close-knit work teams. Internal ventures such as Serengeti Eyewear, the MEMS Unit or NEES Energy were led by small and cohesive multi-disciplinary teams. Multi-project venturing units, such as Procter and Gamble's "CNV", "DSM-NBD" and HP's "IPO" were also led by small, knowledgeable teams of managers and the projects they approved were entrusted to small teams of employees with complementary profiles; 3M and Google rely systematically on small work teams to develop innovative projects. At Gore, the belief that any employee who is able to convince two or three colleagues to work on his/her project should be given permission, time and resources is a core tenet. As a result, self-appointed project teams are commonplace in this company.

Promoting Corporate Entrepreneurship through HR policies

Morris and Jones (1999), Hayton (2005), Wolcott and Lippitz (2007a) and Schmelter et al. (2010) have underlined the important role played by human resources management practices, including staff recruitment, training, compensation and job design, in supporting Corporate Entrepreneurship. Hayton and Kelley (2006) described a list of all the individual competencies required to innovate, broker, champion and sponsor entrepreneurial initiatives within large organisations to show how different HR policies can contribute to their development. Human resources management practices, such as recruitment, staffing and training play a role in several of the cases surveyed.

Selecting "entrepreneurial profiles" is a recurrent practice in our case base. Managers who wish to foster Corporate Entrepreneurship explicitly look for employees who are "self-starters", "creative", "passionate" and "well-connected". The company HomeServe uses a specific questionnaire to try and rate the entrepreneurial orientation of its potential recruits. The staff of "Serengeti Eyewear" were initially selected to include a majority of unconventional, risk-loving profiles. Corporate venturing entities such as HP's "IPO", Lucent's "NVG" or BP's "Office of the CTO" pick their managers carefully and favour unconventional and well-connected "self-starters".

Some HR managers go a step further and set up ambitious training programmes involving hundreds of employees. They are convinced that the main barriers to Corporate Entrepreneurship lie in people's mindsets because employees do not know what Corporate Entrepreneurship is, because they do not think they have the required skills or because they think that acting entrepreneurially would be impossible or insufficiently supported by the existing organisation. Training programmes are designed to help selected employees (often "high potentials") transform their representations, acquire adequate skills and provide them with concrete guidance and tools. Such training programmes can be found at Siemens Nixdorf, Acordia and "FreCo".

Setting up appropriate incentive and reward systems

The importance of proper rewards and incentives has been underlined by various authors (e.g. Kuratko, Montagno and Hornsby, 1990; Hornsby, Kuratko and Montagno, 1999; Morris and Jones, 1999; Thornberry, 2003; Burgelman, 2005; Hayton, 2005; Brazeal, Schenkel and Azriel, 2008) and their specific impact on Corporate Entrepreneurship has been the object of various studies (Block and Ornati, 1987; Sykes, 1992; Lerner, Azulay and Tishler, 2009; Monsen, Patzelt and Saxton, 2010).

Although it appears that many employees engage in Corporate Entrepreneurship without expecting any extrinsic reward, in the longer long-term, they all end up questioning the positive or negative implications of their upward-spiralling commitment. In several cases, what motivates corporate entrepreneurs is the implicit expectation of leading the activity they helped create (e.g. Serengeti Eyewear or Myriad Ideas). At some point, however, the question of incentives does become crucial: incentive and reward systems stimulate potentially interested individuals while sending a signal establishing the legitimacy of entrepreneurial initiatives. There is debate, however, concerning the nature of these rewards and incentives, which is reflected in the lack of homogeneity observed across the various companies studied. One approach consists in granting significant financial rewards (this is the case of Lucent's "New Ventures Group", for example). However, this approach has been shown to generate considerable tension between corporate entrepreneurs and other employees. As a result, many companies, in Europe especially, choose to focus on symbolic rewards through the attribution of modest sums (gifts, bonuses, small percentage of the value generated), trophies and prizes. Finally, a third option consists in tying personal performance appraisal and career prospects to entrepreneurial behaviour and the ability to encourage such behaviour among one's subordinates (e.g. at L'Oréal, 3M, Gore and HomeServe).

Establishing formal evaluation and support procedures for Corporate Entrepreneurship

Contrary to the widely held belief that Corporate Entrepreneurship is all about creativity, project assessment and selection mechanisms play an important role in the implementation of Corporate Entrepreneurship. Kanter and Richardson (1991), Kanter et al. (1991b) and Chesbrough's (2000) in-depth case studies show that transparent and formalised evaluation procedures do indeed constitute the backbone of well-designed new venture divisions and entrepreneurial programmes. Brazeal, Schenkel and Azriel (2008) also underline the need for well-communicated expectations, on the one hand, and adequate evaluation, selection and diffusion mechanisms, on the other. Hayton (2004) ties entrepreneurial performance in SMEs to the existence of formal employee participation programmes.

Sophisticated project evaluation and support procedures have been put in place at Ohio Bell, Xerox Corporation, Procter & Gamble, Lucent Technologies, Schneider Electric, Orange FT France (2) and DSM.

Box 6.1 The New Venture Group: a thorough selection process

In 1995, AT&T spins off its telecommunication equipment division. The entity created as a result, Lucent Technologies, becomes, de facto, the world leader in the sector. Lucent Technologies, with a turnover then of $20 billion, houses the famous Bell laboratories that has an annual budget of close to $3.5 billion. The researchers from these laboratories are behind thousands of inventions and technologies, most of which have never been exploited. The idea then was "to create new business and growth by forming an internal group that would leverage the research function of Bell Labs while operating in a venture capital manner". Because start-ups should be protected from lengthy procedures and existing divisional pressures, a new dedicated entity was constituted. The mission of the "New Ventures Group" (NVG) was "to exploit the Lucent technology so as to create activities that rapidly put innovation on the market and to create a more entrepreneurial environment that will encourage and enable rapidity, teamwork and moderate risk taking". The new entity sets an objective of 20 per cent return on investment.

NVG managers set up a project evaluation and monitoring process covering four stages, the transfer from one to another depending on the use of criteria modelled on those used by venture capitalists. These stages were (1) identification of opportunities; (2) market qualification; (3) marketing; and (4) value realisation.

Identification of opportunities – The NVG staff included 15 or so "business developers" who were responsible for identifying technologies in the group that had promising marketing potential. These "business developers" got the intrapreneurial process underway by submitting a project proposal to the evaluation committee. The proposal had to include (1) an evaluation of the technology; (2) a market study;

(3) a business model; and (4) an investigation into aspects relating to intellectual property. About one proposal in three was accepted by the committee. Business developers were allocated additional resources (one or two people) with whom they tried to improve their understanding of the market potential. If the potential was judged worthwhile and if the technology was developing favourably, the operational division heads were asked if they wish to take on the project under their responsibility. Division heads had first refusal but they were obliged to give a quick response. If they did not answer within the deadlines laid down, the NVG was at liberty to take the project back for itself.

Market qualification – An initial budget of between $50,000 and $100,000 was allocated to the projects that got through the first close examination. A provisional team was set up with members from the laboratories (often the inventors), operational divisions or from outside the company. The business plan was set out, the prototype completed and the concept tested with potential customers. Independent venture capitalists were invited to invest alongside Lucent. The total budget for this qualification stage could go up to $1 million per project. This stage lasted from three to 12 months. The stage finished with the evaluation and review of the business plan by the evaluation committee.

Marketing – The projects that got through this close scrutiny were ready to be marketed. They would therefore need considerable financial resources and the project team had to be capable of attracting outside investors. A company was then created, the definitive team established and the value creation activities initiated. This stage could be interrupted at various intervals by several investor rounds to raise funds of between $1 million and $20 million.

Value realisation – This final stage took place between five and eight years after the project had started. From the viewpoint of the actors involved, it was an essential stage because it enabled them to realise the value that they had generated. The options to be envisaged at this stage were (1) the acquisition of the start-up by Lucent; (2) the sale of the start-up to another company; (3) a floatation; (4) the sale of the technology licences; (5) the purchase of the technology by the start-up; and (6) liquidation.

In March 2001, the New Ventures Group held a portfolio of 20 start-ups exploiting the Bell laboratory technologies. Five start-ups were spun off, three of which generated substantial revenues. The $200 million or so of liquidity generated represented an IRR of 70 per cent.

Source: Adapted from Chesbrough (2000) and Chesbrough and Massaro (2001).

Evaluation processes are generally entrusted with a few dedicated managers who can advise corporate entrepreneurs and introduce them to other significant actors in the organisation who may act as sponsors or expert mentors. Projects get reviewed by committees, which include corporate executives and, often, members of various divisions and functions. Evaluation processes are funnel-shaped with successive stages of increasing stringency (e.g. Kodak's ODI, Lucent's NVG, Schneider Electric's Myriad Ideas, Orange FT IDClic). Selected projects move forward through various review phases leading to the elimination of less attractive projects and increased commitment of the company towards the most promising ones. The final stage of the evaluation process consists in redirecting completed projects towards an exit strategy, an existing division or creating a new operational entity. According to the scope and complexity of the projects being evaluated, going through the various stages can take a few months (Enter-Prize, IDClic) to several years (five to eight years in the case of Lucent Technologies' NVG, up to ten years at DSM's NBD).

Ad hoc time allocation policy

Several authors have emphasised the importance of time in the pursuit of entrepreneurial initiatives (Burgelman, 1984; Pinchot, 1985; Fry, 1987; Brazeal, 1993; Garvin, 2002; Hornsby, Kuratko and Zahra, 2002). Technical and financial resources may be scarce but time is the one resource corporate entrepreneurs cannot do without. Corporate entrepreneurs require time to think, try, fail, learn, interact and experiment.

A "free time" rule is official in firms such as 3M and Google (the 15 per cent rule at 3M where all employees can spend up to 15 per cent of company time on the project of their choice, the 80/20 policy at Google). This "free time" rule plays an important role in establishing a favourable climate, especially when it constitutes a key element of the company's identity, as is the case for 3M and Google.

In summary

☐ Combining a thorough literatur
rate Entrepreneurship implemer
Corporate Entrepreneurship en:
☐ The key enablers we identified a:

(1) Explicit commitment of to
Entrepreneurship
(2) Providing islands of autonor
(3) Improving communication a
(4) Promoting Corporate Entre;
(5) Setting up appropriate incen
Entrepreneurship
(6) Establishing formal Corpora
and support procedures
(7) Time allocation policy

To go further

Read the case in Box 6.2 and draw the list of enablers put in place by 3M to ensure that an entrepreneurial culture is nurtured and that entrepreneurial behaviours become the norm within the company. Are any of the seven key enablers previously identified missing? Can you identify additional enablers? Discuss.

Box 6.2 Mini-case 3M

3M: an entrepreneurial culture since 1902

3M invests, on average, 6 per cent to 7 per cent of its turnover in R&D and has 100 laboratories worldwide. The company masters a hundred or so different technologies, the most important of which are the application of thin layers and adhesives.

To ensure that this investment and know-how generates the greatest possible value, 3M relies on an internal environment that encourages creativity and innovation. First, there is the famous 15 per cent rule that allows employees to devote 15 per cent of their time to a project of their choice. Access to start-up capital is easy and everybody is aware of the procedures. As soon as an idea is considered promising enough, a development team is formed. The project is evaluated on several occasions and its financing is subject to it complying with the criteria covering technical feasibility and economic potential. 3M's philosophy is that of speeding up the stages prior to the test under real conditions, the market being the best judge of an innovative product or service. In fact, one of 3M's mottos is "Make a little, sell a little". The activities that survive this stringent selection process soon become independent business units. These units are meant to grow and become divisions that will, in turn, give rise to new products and business units along the lines of a process similar to that of cellular division. This profuse growth makes it possible to keep up with the company's very ambitious product range renewal objectives (30 per cent of the products have to be less than four years old).

3M is known not only for its very sophisticated innovation culture but also for its performance culture, measured in terms of turnover growth, operating profit as a percentage of turnover and return on invested capital. All the divisions must post very good performances because, according to the CEO, "some of our activities are well established but none has really reached maturity".

3M's structure and culture make it easier to bring together scattered sources of expertise. The junior staff members are told repeatedly that "while the products belong to the divisions, the technologies belong to the company". Everyone is encouraged to develop an informal network that goes beyond the unit they come under. Experts from other divisions are often asked to give their opinion or collaborate on a project. It is common practice for divisions to lend staff to each other. The employees are assessed on their leadership quality that 3M defines as "the ability to lead others down a new path". Numerous prizes and awards are presented each year to the employees who have excelled in their performance and used initiative.

3M has been able to preserve its original culture despite the various crises that it has gone through. The company succeeds in adapting to the demands of an ever more competitive environment without going back on its values. Thus, if the end of the 1980s was marked by a hardening of the selection criteria and a restriction in the number and originality of projects in progress, the 1990s saw a return to the entrepreneurial approach and a re-affirmation that they had got it wrong which, according to the then CEO, was less costly than "the absence of creativity and commitment".

Likewise, in recent years, 3M knew how to find a new lease of life by focusing closely on its customers' needs; 3M redefined its relations with its customers and re-directed its offer towards services. Customer account managers have acquired a prominent position in the new organisation and coordinate all the people and resources needed to meet customer demands, irrespective of the unit they come under. Links that are much more direct unite technology experts and customer managers, all of which make it possible to considerably improve the company's responsiveness.

Source: Adapted from Bartlett and Mohammed (1994, 1995).

Notes

1 These statistics, which focus on the enablers *deliberately* put in place to foster Corporate Entrepreneurship are based on the analysis of 27 cases. The three *spontaneous* Corporate Entrepreneurship cases that are included in our case base (Joline at Polaroid, IBM Rebels and IE at Dow Chemical) have been excluded from the analysis.
2 All the companies and Corporate Entrepreneurship Devices mentioned in this chapter are described and referenced in Appendix 1.

Implementing Corporate Entrepreneurship: Corporate Entrepreneurship Devices

7

As seen in the previous chapter, there exists an abundant literature focusing on specific enablers of Corporate Entrepreneurship. Another important strand of the literature underlines the multiplicity and heterogeneity of corporate entrepreneurship enablers, viewing each of them as distinct but necessary requirements (Kuratko, Montagno and Hornsby, 1990; Hornsby, Kuratko and Montagno, 1999; Zahra, Jennings and Kuratko, 1999; Garvin, 2002; Herbert and Brazeal, 2004; Brazeal, Schenkel and Azriel, 2008; Ireland, Covin and Kuratko, 2009; Kuratko, Covin and Garrett, 2009; Morris et al., 2009). In our view, both perspectives are distant from the realities of Corporate Entrepreneurship, which usually relies on **specific combinations of Corporate Entrepreneurship enablers** deployed to reach particular corporate goals in a given organisational context. These specific combinations of Corporate Entrepreneurship enablers, or "Corporate Entrepreneurship Devices" as we name them, constitute the topic of this chapter.

Corporate Entrepreneurship Devices reflect the goals, context and specificities of the companies setting them up and are consequently quite varied in matters of micro-detail. One could, in fact, argue that no two Corporate Entrepreneurship Devices are exactly similar or have exactly the same impact on employee behaviour and organisational dynamics. However, the close observation of their structure and configuration allows the identification of a few recurrent, well recognisable models. Again, using our rich case database, we were able to identify seven such models. In this chapter, we review each model in detail and describe its impact on the Corporate Entrepreneurship process and its outcomes.

A wide variety of Corporate Entrepreneurship Devices

Corporate Entrepreneurship Devices differ according to:

- Their goals (focused on economic results – focused on human resources management – focused on other goals)
- The type of projects and the level of participation sought (many and varied projects – few and targeted projects; broad participation – selective participation)
- Their level of structural integration in the organisation (independent entity – internal entrepreneurial "pathway")
- Their access to resources (dedicated managers/financial envelope – no earmarked resources)
- The rewards proposed to corporate entrepreneurs (mainly financial – mainly non-financial)

The "Myriad of Ideas" device, set up by a European leader in electrical equipment at the end of 1990s and the "New Venture Group" device, set up by Lucent Technologies[1] at the same time, illustrate this diversity (Table 7.1).

Classifying Corporate Entrepreneurship Devices according to organisational scope and organisational integration

As apparent in the studies of Kanter et al. (1990, 1991a, 1991b), Kanter, Quinn and North (1992) and Stopford and Baden-Fuller (1994) or in Wolcott and Lippitz's (2007a) typology, Corporate Entrepreneurship Devices vary greatly in terms of their organisational **scope**. Some Corporate Entrepreneurship Devices concern just a few individuals working on a single project, whereas others affect several hundred – in some cases several thousand – employees, thus giving rise to a multitude of entrepreneurial projects.

The Corporate Entrepreneurship cases included in our study can be arrayed on a broad continuum ranging from comprehensive to narrow in scope, with considerable implications in terms of resources deployed, organisational configuration and outcomes. Three categories of Corporate Entrepreneurship Devices have been identified along this dimension: (1) *narrow scope* or Single-project Corporate Entrepreneurship Devices, which are

Table 7.1 Two very different Corporate Entrepreneurship Devices

	Myriad of Ideas	The New Venture Group
Purpose of the device	First, to infuse new enthusiasm and dynamism to an organisation worn out by a series of mergers and acquisitions (human resources emphasis). Second, additional revenues.	First, more cash out of the inventions of Bell Laboratories (economic emphasis). Second, fighting the brain drain.
Range of projects and participation	Very wide range, all employees can propose an idea and develop it into a real business or value creating initiative.	Narrow range, high-tech and high economic potential projects, for highly skilled employees only.
Level of organisational integration	The device is an entrepreneurial **pathway** fully integrated in the existing organisation. Corporate entrepreneurs receive guidance and support in the development of their project from a small team of full-time officials and a network of volunteer "sponsors". Corporate entrepreneurs, at least initially, retain their function in the existing organisation.	The New Venture Group is an independent **organisational entity** with its resource envelope, objectives, management systems and support services (legal, accounting, etc.). It brings together Lucent employees who have decided to move to the "other side" and a number of experienced entrepreneurs recruited from outside.
Resources	No financial envelope. Projects are evaluated three times and funded according to pre-set criteria. Their funding is conditional on their value creation potential but also on the reputation of the project leader.	Important financial envelope. Projects are evaluated three times according to transparent criteria. Their funding is conditional on their economic potential.
Rewards	Intrinsic rewards: being autonomous and creative, developing a project from A to Z in the protective bosom of the company. Managing one's own activity if successful.	Important economic incentives. High salaries, "phantom shares" in the start-up but loss of acquired benefits and no turning back to the previous job.

Source: Bouchard (2009IIC), Chesbrough (2000) and Chesbrough and Massaro (2001).

put in place to nurture and fast-track the development of specific projects or business activities and involve a small number of employees – at least initially (e.g. Serengeti Eyewear Division, the MEMS Unit, the "Projet TV sur ADSL"); (2) *intermediate scope* or Multi-project Devices, which aim at fostering an entrepreneurial capability without drastically modifying the existing organisation and usually involve many employees working on several projects, their number, however, never representing a dominant share of the total workforce (e.g. Schneider Electric's Myriad Ideas, Lucent's New Ventures Group, Ohio Bell's "Enter-Prize" programme); and finally, (3) *Comprehensive* Devices, which are meant to align the values and behaviours of the whole workforce with a corporate strategy and culture centred on autonomy, strong personal commitment, responsiveness and innovativeness (e.g. 3M, Gore, HomeServe).

The level of *organisational integration* of Corporate Entrepreneurship Devices is another relevant dimension when trying to identify basic models (Birkinshaw, 1997). The cases examined reveal that the level of integration of Corporate Entrepreneurship Devices strongly affects their day-to-day running and longevity. There are three main configurations: (1) the device is fully *integrated* in the existing organisation, which means that the majority of actors involved in the Corporate Entrepreneurship process belong to, and remain within, pre-existing functions and departments; (2) the device is a *separate* organisational entity, distinct from the rest organisation, with its own staff, strategy and resources; and (3) the device is *hybrid*: corporate entrepreneurs are part of a distinct operational entity whose strategic objectives and project portfolio are established jointly with the managers of other parts of the organisation.

Single-project devices

Our case base includes seven Single-project Devices: Barilla's DPF, Orange FT's Projet TV sur ADSL, Schlumberger's MEMS Unit, Corning's Serengeti Eyewear Division, NEES Energy Venture, Merlin-Gérin Foundry Business and Nestlé's NCS (Nespresso). The comparison of their constitutive elements showed remarkable similarities. Because Single-project Devices are small and self-contained, the corresponding model was named "Entrepreneurial Cell".

Model 1: The "Entrepreneurial Cell"

"Entrepreneurial Cells" are separate entities created ad hoc to pursue one single opportunity considered by senior management as divergent or risky, but potentially attractive and/or urgent. Once an Entrepreneurial Cell has reached its strategic goal, it can be spun-off, merged into the existing organisation or become a new operating division. Also called "individual units" (Brazeal, 1993), Entrepreneurial Cells typically involve small teams of people who work in close connection and report directly to senior management. Compact and agile, Entrepreneurial Cells can avoid some of the usual organisational roadblocks and thus introduce radical innovation and / or reach market faster. Entrepreneurial Cells have their own strategy and space (usually away from the parent company's offices) and their own human, financial and technical resources, but they also take advantage, when possible, of the parent company's resources and competencies (legal and accounting services, HR management, R&D, reputation, etc.). Members of Entrepreneurial Cells are chosen on the basis of their functional and technical expertise and qualities such as risk-taking, adaptability and proactiveness. In many cases, the leaders of Entrepreneurial Cells are individuals with strong entrepreneurial profiles.

Entrepreneurial Cells pursuing viable business concepts have proven successful in a variety of environments (cf. Orange FT, Nestlé, Corning). Their success, however, is highly dependent on the steady support of senior management, sometimes over extended periods of time. The success of Entrepreneurial Cells is also dependent on the organisational savvy and political agility of their members. Given these prerequisites, Entrepreneurial Cells constitute low cost, low risk Corporate Entrepreneurship Devices that can help large and rigid companies accelerate the pace and widen the scope of their innovation.

Multi-project Devices

There are 14 *intermediate* or "Multi-project" Corporate Entrepreneurship Devices in our case base. All 14 involved a significant number of employees (from a few hundred to a few thousand) and aimed at **fostering Corporate Entrepreneurship without noticeably modifying the existing organisation**. A more detailed analysis of their configuration led to the identification of four distinct models, which we will now review.

Model 2: The "Entrepreneurial Pathway"

The "Entrepreneurial Pathway" is a device designed to stimulate an internal dynamic of change, resulting in renewed employee commitment and motivation, as well as improved corporate performance, without challenging existing organisational structures and processes. Most of the actors involved in

"Entrepreneurial Pathways" – corporate entrepreneurs, experts, champions, sponsors and mentors – continue to perform their regular jobs and contribute to projects on a volunteer basis, on top of their regular jobs.

Entrepreneurial Pathways provide employees with easily accessible contact points to help them discuss, test and develop their entrepreneurial projects. They rely on formal yet simple project screening and support procedures and a system of symbolic (prizes, trophies, etc.) or small financial rewards. Entrepreneurial Pathways are generally sponsored by top executives and widely publicised throughout the firm. Special events showcasing innovative projects and celebrating successful corporate entrepreneurs are put in place. These events contribute to increasing the Pathway's visibility and to maintaining its appeal over time.

Entrepreneurial Pathways are meant to be open to all employees and welcome both ambitious and modest projects. They have relatively low running costs, but require a competent and creative managing team to keep them going, as well as the unwavering support of senior managers. We closely examined four Entrepreneurial Pathways: Ohio Bell's "Enter-Prize", Orange FT's "IDClic", Schneider Electric's "Myriad Ideas" and Eastman Kodak's "OI and NOD". The first two endured successfully over a significant period of time, whereas the third, after promising beginnings, failed to get the support of the new top management team. As Kanter et al. (1991b) observed, Eastman Kodak's "OI and NOD", the fourth device, had only a minor impact on the firm's culture and performance. The filters put in place to select innovative projects were too stringent and not enough was done regarding communication on innovative projects and celebrating innovators.

When well designed and well managed on a day-to-day basis, Entrepreneurial Pathways can contribute effectively to motivate employees and to nourish creativity and personal commitment at all levels of the corporation. However, they can easily fall prey to the organisational dysfunctions they are supposed to alleviate; that is, bureaucratic procedures and overly stringent selection criteria.

Model 3: The "Entrepreneurial Division"

The Entrepreneurial Division is a device designed to reinforce the firm's internal growth and innovation rate by better leveraging its intangible assets (inventions, original product and process technologies, unique competences, brands, etc.). It aims at developing new business lines with significant potential (over M$100 in annual revenues in some cases). Entrepreneurial Divisions can also fulfil other goals such as retaining innovative, highly talented employees and positioning the corporation as an innovation leader. Entrepreneurial Divisions are popular with firms competing in technology-intensive industries, where R&D spending is significant. We identified four Entrepreneurial Divisions in our case base: Xerox Technology Ventures, Lucent Technologies' New Ventures Group, Procter & Gamble's Corporate New Ventures and DSM's New Business Development.

Innovation specialists agree that "start-ups need to be surrounded by high protective walls in order to avoid being crushed by day-to-day routine operations" (Day et al., 2001) and the Entrepreneurial Division plays this role. To reach its ambitious goals, it operates as a separate organisational entity with its own financial and human resources and generally reports directly to top management. The management of the Entrepreneurial Division selects and manages its project portfolio (usually innovative concepts or products that operational divisions find too risky or poorly aligned with their strategic goals), defines its own performance criteria and management rules and protects its staff from undue organisational pressure and the tyranny of short-term results. The employees of Entrepreneurial Divisions are expected to behave like real entrepreneurs and may, in return, benefit from attractive compensation schemes.

Entrepreneurial Divisions are typically run by relatively small teams of experienced managers with complementary skills and broad networks extending inside and outside the company and whose responsibility is to scout attractive ideas and technologies, assemble ad hoc teams of developers and help these teams get through the various stages of the venturing process, generally under the supervision of a board of top executives. Projects are selected, vetted and moved forward in several steps, based on strict evaluation criteria inspired by venture capitalists' practices. This multi-stage selection process constitutes an effective control tool for limiting the risks inherent in exploratory activities. Entrepreneurial Divisions can also be quite effective in stimulating innovativeness and top-line growth, but frequently struggle with organisational and internal politics issues. Although designed to be self-standing, Entrepreneurial Divisions often depend on the parent company for political support and on operating divisions for product commercialisation: when Entrepreneurial Divisions' managers neglect to cultivate good relations with these stakeholders, they may face a lack of cooperation and even rejection at later stages. Perceived differences in treatment between those who work for the Entrepreneurial Division and other employees may also raise issues of equity. Furthermore, the practice of dedicating valuable human resources and managerial attention to ventures that eventually get spun off can be seen as questionable. These issues may result in serious tensions and conflicts, sometimes leading to the disbanding of the Entrepreneurial Division. To be lasting and effective, Entrepreneurial Divisions require careful design and monitoring, especially regarding the management of their organisational, strategic and operational ties with the rest of the organisation.

Model 4: The "Entrepreneurial Booster"

The Entrepreneurial Booster is a multi-project Corporate Entrepreneurship Device that shares many characteristics with the Entrepreneurial Division but maintains, thanks to various mechanisms, a strong organic link with the rest of the organisation. We found four cases corresponding to this model in our database: Raytheon's "New Product Centre", Nokia's "New Venture Organization", HP's "Innovation Program Office" and BP's "Office of the Chief Technology Officer".

Typically, the Entrepreneurial Booster is an organisational entity that is autonomous in terms of its funding and daily management, but whose strategic goals and project portfolio are established jointly with senior operations managers from the parent company. It is not positioned as a self-contained entity, but as a dedicated "organ" in close relation with the mainstream organisation: it does not own the projects it develops, but nurtures them for a while on behalf of the firm's other operating units. The functions of the Entrepreneurial Booster are to (1) take risks that existing divisions cannot/do not want to take and (2) accelerate product-development life cycles. Entrepreneurial projects are developed by small, dedicated teams, which often include the idea generator. Teams get disbanded once projects have reached a critical stage (proven concept, successful pilot, etc.) and are being passed on to operational units. Employees involved in Entrepreneurial Boosters are considered experts in project and business development, not necessarily as "entrepreneurs".

This Corporate Entrepreneurship Device is particularly attractive insofar as it appears to minimise conflicts and tensions while providing an environment conducive to the development of "divergent" and innovative projects. The success of Entrepreneurial Boosters greatly depends on the talent and connections of their management team, their ability to strike a balance between autonomy and integration and to convince operating divisions of their usefulness. This observation is consistent with the findings of Kanter et al. (1991a), Heller (1999) and Burgers et al. (2009) regarding the importance of balancing the autonomy of new venture units with adequate integration mechanisms. Overall, this Corporate Entrepreneurship Device appears stable and enduring over time.

Model 5: The "Entrepreneurial Mission"

The "Entrepreneurial Mission" is a multi-project Corporate Entrepreneurship Device that relies mostly on intangible managerial resources and actions (senior management declarations, communication plans, training programmes), initially targeting a selected group of employees with a view to slowly and progressively transforming the corporate "mindset". The Entrepreneurial Mission rests on the premise that (1) obstacles to Corporate Entrepreneurship are mostly due to employees' inadequate representations and that (2) infusing Corporate Entrepreneurship across the organisation depends largely on imitation and emulation. The device is designed to train and convert a selected group of managers (the "missionaries") in the hope that they will then inspire entrepreneurial behaviours thanks to their example and leadership. Although Entrepreneurial Missions are commonplace, they are little documented. Our findings rely on the analysis of two case studies ("Freco" and Siemens Nixdorf) and our own experience as Executive Programme trainers.

Entrepreneurial Missions involve development programmes that usually combine theoretical teachings and teamwork on actual entrepreneurial projects. Participants are encouraged to apply the knowledge and skills acquired during training and tap into the network they have built to promote their project. They are assigned sponsors among the firm's senior management and invited to present their results to a committee of top executives.

The Entrepreneurial Mission has a number of pitfalls and some of them have been discussed in Thornberry (2003). One of them is a direct consequence of the heterogeneity of participants' profiles and goals: while some of them display a truly entrepreneurial spirit and want to develop it further, others are more interested in acquiring general management skills and others simply comply with the requirements of their manager. Finally, although many participants come out of the training process motivated and convinced, they often face serious organisational obstacles when they try to behave like entrepreneurs. To be effective, Entrepreneurial Missions should be reinforced thanks to Corporate Entrepreneurship enablers such as general awareness campaigns targeting senior managers and the organisation at large, formal and transparent evaluation and support procedures, appropriate incentive schemes and so on.

"Comprehensive" Devices

There are seven "comprehensive" Corporate Entrepreneurship Devices in our case base. These Devices are meant to align the values and behaviours of the **whole** workforce of a company with a corporate strategy and culture centred on proactiveness, innovativeness, autonomy and strong personal commitment. A thorough analysis of these Devices allowed us to identify two distinct models: the "Incubator Organisation" and the "Hive Organisation".

Model 6: "The Incubator Organisation"

The "Incubator Organisation" combines a rich mix of levers that constitutes the very fabric of the organisation. It is undoubtedly the most ambitious and thoroughgoing of all the models reviewed. Three firms have adopted this model: 3M, Google and W.L. Gore & Associates.

The intent of companies who opt for the model is to infuse all their managers with the kind of attributes conducive to innovation, risk-taking and strong personal commitment. In order to do so, they deploy a broad and coherent array of Corporate Entrepreneurship enablers: motivating statements and concrete top management actions, discretionary time allowance, accessible seed money and technical expertise, clear and transparent vetting procedures and rules and incentive and reward systems reinforcing the other measures and tools. In spite of their size, these companies keep a flat and decentralised structure and rely on small, close-knit work teams to develop innovative projects. Employees' creativity is encouraged and then adequately channelled via informal and formal selection and prioritisation procedures. The coherence between the various elements of the organisation contributes to creating a safe and stimulating environment for corporate entrepreneurs and a corporate climate conducive to risk-taking, experimentation and horizontal interactions.

Should all companies eager to encourage employee initiative and innovation adopt this organisational model? There are reasons to doubt it. The three companies who adopted it are well known for their focus on new product development and technological leadership: strategic orientations that are particularly fitting with bottom-up innovation and the generalisation of entrepreneurial practices. They compete in heterogeneous industries characterised by the existence of many niches and an entrepreneurial organisation helps them introduce new products and target new client segments quickly and effectively. Companies competing in high-volume industries with long innovation cycles, or facing major technology disruptions, might not find this organisational model relevant. In their case, a top-down innovation process is probably more appropriate.

Model 7: The "Entrepreneurial Hive"

We found three companies corresponding to this Corporate Entrepreneurship Device in our case base: Acordia, HomeServe and SAS. All three belong to the service sector, and for these companies, the adoption of entrepreneurial values and attitudes by their employees, those in contact with clients in particular, is a critical success factor because it directly impacts client satisfaction and revenue generation.

The Entrepreneurial Hive aims first and foremost at fostering initiative taking, proactiveness and accountability at all levels of the organisation and increasing employees' direct contribution to growth and profit. Like the Incubator Organisation, the Entrepreneurial Hive is a deliberate attempt at preventing bureaucratisation by favouring a flat and decentralised organisational structure. The Entrepreneurial Hive deploys an array of Corporate Entrepreneurship enablers, such as the strong implication of top management expressed through powerful communication campaigns and HR policies – hiring, staffing and training – that promote entrepreneurial values and behaviours, as well as performance measurement and incentive systems that monitor and reward entrepreneurial behaviour at all levels. Other enablers such as "time to dabble" and formal project evaluation and support procedures are not emphasised. As a result, the Entrepreneurial Hive seems more effective in energising employees and fuelling the growth of existing activities than in stimulating radical innovation and diversification. Overall, this model appears effective and enduring over time.

Conclusion

The identification of seven very different Corporate Entrepreneurship Devices shows that there is no one-fits-all solution, but a range of best implementation approaches. The success of Corporate Entrepreneurship implementation attempts greatly depends on the capacity of concerned managers to identify the appropriate enablers and combine them into Devices that are well aligned with the firm's capabilities and goals.

Based on our observations, coherence and comprehensiveness play a key role in ensuring success. The various parts that constitute a Corporate Entrepreneurship Device should complement and reinforce each other. The Entrepreneurial Mission, for instance, is a somewhat fragile model because it is not supported with appropriate complementary enablers. Many Corporate Entrepreneurship implementation attempts fail because of a lack of alignment between top management's discourse and allocated resources. Without adequate resources, the various enablers that constitute the Corporate Entrepreneurship Device cannot be managed properly and soon the dynamic generated comes to a halt. Another key success factor, as highlighted by Kanter et al. (1990), relates to the strength of the links between the Corporate Entrepreneurship Device and the rest of the organisation. A fine and dynamic balance has to be struck between autonomy and integration.

In summary

☐ Attempts at encouraging Corporate Entrepreneurship have an organisational translation, which we label "Corporate Entrepreneurship Devices". These Devices can be arrayed on a broad continuum ranging from comprehensive to narrow in **scope**, with considerable implications in terms of resources deployed, organisational configuration and outcomes.

☐ The level of **organisational integration** of Corporate Entrepreneurship Devices is another relevant dimension when trying to identify basic models. The cases examined reveal that the level of **organisational integration** of Corporate Entrepreneurship Devices strongly affects their day-to-day running and longevity.

☐ Figure 7.1 positions each of the models along these two critical dimensions.

☐ The success of Corporate Entrepreneurship implementation attempts depends on:

(1) The choice of an appropriate model (given the company's objectives and characteristics)

(2) The combination of various "enablers" into a coherent whole

(3) Adequate resources and effective day-to-day management of the various "parts" of the Corporate Entrepreneurship Device

To go further

Identify one company that is purposefully encouraging Corporate Entrepreneurship. Briefly describe the organisational device they have implemented to reach their goals. Identify the enablers they have put in place, referring to the list of enablers that appears in the previous chapter. Qualify their Corporate Entrepreneurship Device in terms of scope and integration. To what model does it correspond?

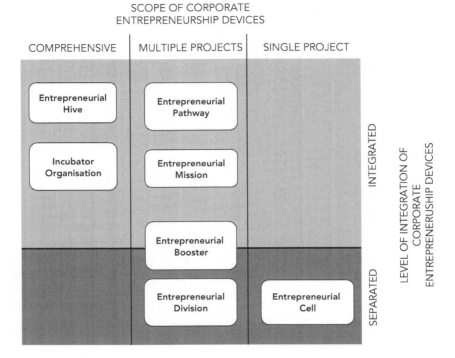

Figure 7.1 A map of Corporate Entrepreneurship Devices

Note

1 All the companies and Corporate Entrepreneurship Devices mentioned in this chapter are described and referenced in Appendix 1.

Implementing Corporate Entrepreneurship: the underlying design principles

8

Introduction

In the previous chapter, we reviewed several approaches to implementing Corporate Entrepreneurship focusing on the managerial tools and organisational devices that companies design and put in place to encourage Corporate Entrepreneurship and reach their specific goals. We were able to identify seven basic Enabling Tools and seven models of Corporate Entrepreneurship Devices and endeavoured to describe and assess each of them. In this concluding chapter, we will pursue our study of Corporate Entrepreneurship implementation, now focusing on the underlying design principles that lie at the heart of all Corporate Entrepreneurship implementation attempts.

The mini-case in Box 8.1 provides a preview of these principles.

From the mini-case, it is obvious that "autonomy" constitutes one of the underlying principles when implementing Corporate Entrepreneurship.

A second important principle is related to "extra motivation and commitment". When senior managers deliberately encourage Corporate Entrepreneurship, it is because they expect extra effort and commitment on the part of corporate entrepreneurs. And they get it! The DPF managers and employees felt they had a special mission and put enormous energy and creativity into their job. They fought many battles and surmounted major obstacles – internally and externally, thanks to their unwavering commitment to the team and the project. The DPF team was not given access to sufficient resources and had to be very creative to obtain what it needed. For example, the managers of the DPF used their own personal contacts to access market data and perform product tests for free or at very low cost. Because the parent company did not want to invest in manufacturing equipment for the DPF, the team decided to use contract packers, thus challenging the company's tenets in matters of manufacturing policy.

Box 8.1 The "Divisione Prodotti Freschi" case

In the late 1970s, Barilla, the number one Italian pasta producer, had narrow growth and profit perspectives and its owners were pushing for diversification. Fresh bakery products were identified by Barilla's management as a highly attractive but a relatively risky business opportunity that relied, for the most part, on resources and competencies that the company did not have. A new Division was formed and a small task force was put in charge of creating the new business from scratch. The "Divisione Prodotti Freschi" (DPF) was organisationally and physically separated from the rest of the company and had almost no contact with it. The small team, which occupied a few rooms on the first floor of a disused factory, was made up of executives and employees who were difficult to fit according to the criteria in force at the company. One experienced marketing director recruited from the competition completed the picture. The financial resources placed at the disposal of the team were practically nil: this was consistent with the lack of commitment of the senior management and lack of support of the "mainstream" who did not find the team members to be very serious! No particular inducements were provided to corporate entrepreneurs apart from the remote prospect of managing a division if they were successful. Interference from top management was limited and control was exercised mainly through severe budgetary constraints. Fortunately, this disparate group was united by an intense desire for success and a strong entrepreneurial spirit. During the first two years of the venture's existence, the most unthinkable means were imagined and implemented by the DPF team, which neither the lack of money nor the lack of support seemed to affect. The team succeeded in obtaining market data without buying studies, finding simple solutions to apparently insoluble food preservation problems and producing without productive capacity and selling without a sales force. The team even subcontracted its billing, resulting in a 75 per cent economy saving. The team, unknowingly, was inventing and testing a new business model that, years later, would be theorised under the name of "virtual enterprise".

At the end of three years, a very profitable new activity was born: its turnover was lower than that of the other main division, but its profitability as a percentage of sales and in absolute value was higher. The value chain of the new business was as different as possible from the traditional value chain but, thanks to the very small capital it entailed, was remarkably profitable and flexible. The new activity was, in fact, so significant that it soon became the "second leg" of the company. At that time, new offices were being built and the DPF was invited to join the rest of the company. The managers of the DPF were now required to comply with standard procedures and rules, but they succeeded in maintaining a great strategic and operational autonomy.

Being deprived of resources, or being granted resources very progressively and conditionally – what we label "resource discipline" – constitutes the third underlying design principle of Corporate Entrepreneurship implementation. Limiting and disciplining corporate entrepreneurs' access to resources is a control tool in the hands of the hierarchy, which, in this way, can balance the autonomy it has to concede. An indirect but powerful consequence of "Resource Discipline" is that it puts the motivation and creativity of corporate entrepreneurs under test and often pushes them to develop low cost, non-conventional solutions.

Reviewing the cases in our database, we find that these underlying design principles were involved in almost all of them (25/27). Each company, however, uniquely interprets and adapts them. We also note that the application of these principles does not necessarily translate into positive results: in several instances (7/27), it led to mixed or negative results. "Autonomy", "Extra Motivation" and "Resource Discipline" should therefore be viewed as necessary but insufficient conditions for the successful implementation of Corporate Entrepreneurship.

Let us now review each underlying design principle in detail (see also Figure 8.1).

The "Autonomy" principle

The links between innovation and freedom, as well as those between business building and self-determination, are well ascertained (Bird, 1988; Katz and Gartner, 1988). It is not surprising therefore that *autonomy*, normally restricted in large organisations, is seen by many as the critical dimension of the independent entrepreneurial process (Lumpkin and Dess, 1996) and the one that all attempts at implementing Corporate Entrepreneurship should encourage and embed (Burgelman, 1983ASQ; Siegel, Siegel and McMillan, 1988).

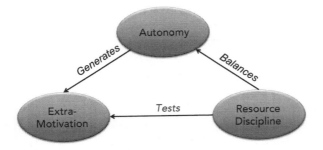

Figure 8.1 The underlying design principles of Corporate Entrepreneurship implementation

Creating a separate entity

In a number of Corporate Entrepreneurship implementation attempts, autonomy is ensured thanks to the creation of a separate entity. The entity is separated *organisationally*, which means it is not accountable to existing operating units, does not depend on them for resources and disposes of an expense and investment envelope. Frequently, the entity is also *physically* separated from the rest of the organisation: Barilla's DPF, for example, was located in an old building a few miles away from the company's main office.

Very often, the entity is *culturally* distinct form the rest of the organisation. Marked differences in the way people work and behave, as well as in the way they are evaluated and rewarded can be observed: the work climate of Barilla's DPF was informal in order to encourage creativity and exchange, which stood in sharp contrast with the company's dominant relational mode. In entrepreneurial entities, controls and procedures are less pervasive and short-term results imperative somewhat dampened: money is "patient". The differences are particularly exacerbated when entrepreneurial entities adopt, like Lucent Technology's NVG, the values, norms and procedures of Venture Capital structures (cf. Box 6.2).

Separation, which is supposed to allow corporate entrepreneurs to pursue their project freely and successfully, can also have negative consequences. A list of some of the problems reported in the cases we analysed is shown in Table 8.1.

Separation can easily lead to **isolation**. As entrepreneurial entities are rarely completely independent from the rest of the organisation, they can greatly suffer from organisational isolation. Isolation can be fatal if it cuts the entrepreneurial entity from strategic information flows about the internal environment, technologies or markets, or if it limits its access to critical

Table 8.1 Implementing Corporate Entrepreneurship: some of the issues raised by organisational separation

Case study	Separate entrepreneurial entity	Key issues
Barilla	The "Divisione Prodotti Freschi" (DPF)	No major issues
Raytheon	The "New Product Center" (NPC)	No major issues
Eastman Kodak	The "New Opportunity Development Office" (NOD)	Mainstream/newstream tensions due to different expectations and levels of success. Refusal to confront constructively led to inevitable tensions. Managerial attrition.
Xerox Corporation	The "Xerox Technology Ventures" (XTV)	Initially, the existing operating units perceived XTV as a competitor that appropriated their technologies and engineers. After one XTV venture was repurchased by Xerox, the entity started to be perceived more positively.
Procter and Gamble	The "Corporate New Ventures" (CNV)	Finding a "home" to produce and market the products it invented and developed.
Lucent Technologies	The "New Venture Group" (NVG)	Initially, getting support from the rest of the company. Cultural clash. Perceived by some as fostering an unhealthy competition within the organisation and reproached for not being transparent. Getting recognition from financial analysts for its achievements.

Source: Cf. Appendix 1.

resources. Isolated entrepreneurial entities can experience great difficulty convincing existing operating divisions to reintegrate new activities that are ready to be mass-produced and commercialised. Similarly, if they find themselves in a delicate situation due to a decreasing commitment on the part of senior management, isolated entrepreneurial entities will not benefit from the support of other divisions and will have to fight for their survival on their own.

Choosing one's own goals

Independent entrepreneurs have complete latitude to select both their goals and their means. Many Corporate Entrepreneurship Devices initially attempt to reproduce this state of affair by limiting *a priori* constraints as much as possible: corporate entrepreneurs should be free to decide both the "what" and the "how". The desire to offer maximum latitude to corporate entrepreneurs is apparent in company statements such as "we want to exploit our technologies in any way that makes business sense" and "we are willing to encourage any idea as long as it is a good business idea". Unfortunately, because it allows corporate entrepreneurs to pursue goals that are sometimes disconnected from those of the company, this complete freedom can have negative consequences.

By pursuing strategically unrelated projects, corporate entrepreneurs can weaken their personal position within the organisation and contribute to diminishing the strategic relevance of Corporate Entrepreneurship and, consequently, its legitimacy. While strategic alignment is seldom mentioned as a key performance indicator at the onset of Corporate Entrepreneurship implementation attempts, it tends to acquire more and more weight as the experiment unfolds. At the end of a three-year period, the "Myriad Ideas" programme was criticised on account of its lack of strategic focus that had led, according to the new top management, to a waste of resources and energy.

The clarification and communication to all employees of the domain within which exploration is legitimate can help reduce this risk (Figure 8.2). The pursuit of strategically aligned projects eliminates a potential source of conflict and uncertainty, which allows corporate entrepreneurs to focus on reaching their goals in the most effective, albeit unorthodox, ways. Because the goals it pursued were approved by all, Barilla's DPF suffered limited hierarchical encroachment and was never strongly questioned by the rest of the organisation in spite of its marked work style differences and unorthodox choice of means.

Rethinking the "Autonomy" principle

The problems associated with the "Autonomy" principle had been identified by Corporate Entrepreneurship researchers early on. In fact, one of the major conclusions of past research is that, in order to be successful, Corporate Entrepreneurship Devices should be designed so as to balance autonomy and integration (Kanter et al., 1990; Day et al., 2001; Morris et al., 2009).

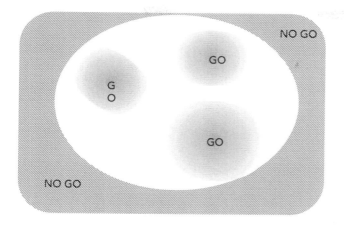

Figure 8.2 Channelling Corporate Entrepreneurship initiatives through clear communication of strategic priorities and off limit areas

How can this objective be reached? The literature underlines the importance of maintaining or establishing proper communication channels between the entrepreneurial entity and the rest of the organisation, as well as including mainstream managers in "newstream" governing boards to ensure their support to the entrepreneurial entity. It also suggests that the level of autonomy and separation of corporate entrepreneurs should correspond to precise and well-ascertained needs and evolve with the maturity of projects.

We believe the key lesson that can be learned from Corporate Entrepreneurship implementation cases is that the autonomy of corporate entrepreneurs is not a given but a rare resource that is conceded by the organisation and needs to be continuously (re)negotiated. Therefore, the autonomy/integration dilemma cannot be solved via structural arrangements (design solution) only, but requires the mastery of a complex social interaction process. Autonomy being scarce and costly, corporate entrepreneurs should clarify the type and extent of autonomy they really need and accept compromises, while giving up on less essential aspects of their endeavour.

The "Extra Motivation" principle

The powerful motivation that allows independent entrepreneurs to put in so much heart, effort and creativity, as well as to pursue their goals with determination and adapt constantly, is definitely a feature that managers of large companies, confronted with low morale and organisational apathy, dream of capturing. Motivation and innovation are closely connected – great motivation is necessary to overcome the difficulties and doubts tied to innovation but innovating is, in itself, highly motivating. The virtuous circle only needs to be sparked.

The motivation of independent entrepreneurs depends on several factors: intrinsic factors – building a new business is in itself very exciting – and extrinsic ones, such as the prospect of acquiring wealth, autonomy and prestige (Naffziger, Hornsby and Kuratko, 1994). In order to instil the motivation of independent entrepreneurs to their employees, some corporations set up reward systems that attempt to combine both dimensions. Most Corporate Entrepreneurship Devices heavily rely on intrinsic rewards: the appeal of developing a project from A to Z, testing oneself and being able to "make a difference" (Frohman, 1997). They add to these the possibility of working in a stimulating, informal environment, company recognition under various forms and, sometimes, financial incentives (see Table 8.2). Although a lack of proper financial incentives has been evoked by some authors (Block and Ornati, 1987), to explain the failure of Corporate Entrepreneurship implementation attempts, it is clear from the cases at hand that corporate entrepreneurs can be highly motivated in absence of any such rewards.

The "Extra-Motivation" backlash and how to avoid it

Looking at the cases at hand, one observes that, in spite of their imperfections, the inducement mechanisms set up to foster Corporate Entrepreneurship work remarkably well. In all the cases analysed, companies managed to elicit a great deal of enthusiasm and involvement on the part of employees. Many employees came up with innovative business ideas and a significant number of them wholeheartedly engaged in the long and uncertain process of business building. In a number of cases, the early phases of the experiment were coloured by strong positive emotions, which participants vividly remember. However, the "Extra Motivation" that Corporate Entrepreneurship generates does not always get transformed into extra performance.

When corporate entrepreneurs engage in risky and demanding activities, they do so on the basis of a psychological contract with the organisation (Rousseau, 1995). Corporate entrepreneurs have tacit expectations concerning what will happen during – in terms of help and support – and after the venture – in terms of rewards, recognition and reinsertion should the necessity arise. If these expectations are not met, bad feelings will be directly

Table 8.2 Corporate Entrepreneurship Devices: incentives and rewards

Case Study	Rewards
Raytheon	Intrinsic rewards; informal, technologically excellent work environment; internal and external recognition
Barilla	Intrinsic rewards; friendly informal work environment; prospect of managing a new division
Eastman Kodak	Intrinsic rewards; prospect of managing one's own activity inside or outside the company
Scandinavian Airlines System	Intrinsic rewards
Ohio Bell	Intrinsic rewards and internal recognition ($10,000 to $30,000 prizes are attributed to year best projects)
Acordia Inc.	Intrinsic rewards and yearly bonus based on individual performance; prospect of running a new division
3M	Intrinsic rewards; best projects awards and informal recognition; career progression tied to entrepreneurial accomplishments; prospect of leading a new division
Siemens Nixdorf Informations systeme	Intrinsic rewards; high-level training; career booster
Xerox Corporation	Intrinsic rewards; prospect of managing one's own business and/or owning shares of a future public company
Procter & Gamble	Intrinsic rewards; friendly, informal work environment
Lucent Technologies	Intrinsic and financial rewards; attractive work environment
Schneider Electric	Intrinsic rewards; visibility; prospect of running and owning one's own business under the sponsorship of the company

Source: Cf. Appendix 1.

proportional to the initial level of motivation and involvement. Demoralised corporate entrepreneurs who believe, for good or bad reasons, that their company has not respected its part of the deal are unfortunately not a rarity. A flawed or excessively stringent selection process can also turn off initially enthusiastic participants. When approvals are too slow, funds too hard to get, when too many people have a say and too many conditions have to be met, the internal venturing process turns into a hurdle race that eliminates all but the most resilient. Corporate entrepreneurs sometimes get caught in the undertow and suffer the consequences of the company's decreasing commitment to Corporate Entrepreneurship just as their personal prospects and motivation are reaching a high point. When companies withdraw their assistance at the very last stage of the business development process, the effects can be devastating. Finally, in case of failure, corporate entrepreneurs can find themselves in an uncomfortable position and feel obliged to leave the company.

The departure of corporate entrepreneurs has negative consequences for the company that undergoes, as a result, a loss in both human and social capital. The loss in human capital can be harmful, especially in a tight labour market, but the loss in social capital – "the goodwill that is engendered by the fabric of social relations and that can be mobilized to facilitate action" (Adler and Kwon, 2002) – can be even more damaging (Dess and Shaw, 2001). Corporate entrepreneurs are social capital generators *par excellence* and their departure can leave a big hole in the social fabric of the company. In effect, corporate entrepreneurs create and maintain extended networks of trusted relations within and outside the corporation to obtain resources, build support and gain legitimacy (Dougherty and Hardy, 1996; Greene, Brush and Hart, 1999). They broker relationships between distant departments, filling the "organisational holes" that result from defective communication channels (Burt, 1992) and become agents of organisational learning (Floyd and Woolridge, 1999; Zahra, Nielsen and Bogner, 1999; Friedman, 2002). When they leave, critical links are severed and informal value generating processes are dropped and forgotten. Corporate entrepreneurs sometimes bring along with them their most trusted colleagues (Cappelli, 2000), causing even greater damage to the social fabric of the company.

In order to avoid a damaging "Extra Motivation" backlash, the first preoccupation of those who wish to encourage Corporate Entrepreneurship should be to ensure the sustained commitment of senior management to the experiment and its participants. They should also carefully manage the expectations of the actors involved. Realistic messages should be communicated to top management as to what benefits they can expect in terms of additional revenues, innovation, time-to-market and so on, as well as what encouraging Corporate Entrepreneurship will cost in terms of financial resources and managerial talent. Employees' expectations in terms of support and rewards should be clarified and the elaboration of an explicit agreement tying the company to each corporate entrepreneur should probably become an integral part of the venture approval and support process.

The "Resource Discipline" principle

Independent entrepreneurs are autonomous and motivated, but also *disciplined* by tough external constraints. Market forces and resource limitations select out "weak" business projects and compel entrepreneurs to be efficient, adaptive and value-oriented.

Similarly, most Corporate Entrepreneurship Devices include a discipline component, if only to balance the autonomy granted to corporate entrepreneurs. In most cases, discipline is imposed by **limiting resource availability and/or making it conditional to specific performance requirements**. From the standpoint of the company, Resource Discipline helps reduce the risk of making costly blunders and encourages a more frugal use of resources in the process of product and business development, thus reducing the cost of innovation. If projects cost less and can be discontinued at any moment, the company is able to pursue more projects simultaneously, thus increasing variety, flexibility and the probability of success measured by the number and significance of new viable businesses.

The Discipline of Scarcity

In many of the cases surveyed, the resources formally available to corporate entrepreneurs are few and hard to get. Scarcity prohibits waste and encourages creativity at all levels (Stevenson and Gumpert, 1985). Faced with strong restrictions, corporate entrepreneurs become good at locating and obtaining, often for free, underused resources both inside and outside the company. They are also excellent at finding new, more economical suppliers and value chain configurations. Finally, penury discourages the creation of complex and rigid organisations: contrary to the company's traditional independence posture and because it disposed of a very limited investment budget, Barilla's DPF outsourced key functions such as manufacturing, outbound logistics and selling. It also outsourced some administrative tasks, reducing their costs by 75 per cent. As its turnover increased, the DPF maintained a restrictive hiring policy. These decisions had a major impact on the DPF's operating profit and return on investment, which ended up significantly higher than those of the parent company.

But scarcity can also be damaging. Corporate entrepreneurs are not always able to access "free resources" or to "invent" lower cost alternatives and can be starved to death by corporate stinginess. Interesting but poorly advocated

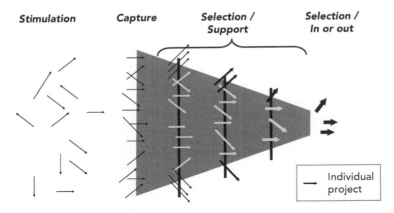

Stimulation **Capture** **Selection / Support** **Selection / In or out**

Individual project

Figure 8.3 The project selection/support funnel

projects can get killed because they are denied seed money in the order of a few thousand dollars.

The Discipline of Conditionality

Many Corporate Entrepreneurship Devices aim at replicating a "natural selection" process and bet on the "law of large numbers" to ensure their success. As one manager explains: "if we can generate a thousand ideas, we will be able to test a hundred. Out of those hundred, twenty might prove a success and five could become the core businesses of tomorrow". In order to emulate the natural selection process, the Corporate Entrepreneurship project selection process usually combines a wide-open idea generation and entry phase with a stringent selection process that funds projects conditionally and in various stages (see Figure 8.3). *A priori* restrictions are limited in order to foster variety, originality and participation. However, this wide-open entry is compensated by strict assessment procedures that aim at rapidly eliminating poor ideas and progressively allocating resources to "good" ideas.

Such a "stage by stage" project funding process helps companies and individuals tailor their level of commitment to the prospects that uncertainty reduction progressively delineates, reducing risks for both parties. It turns projects into "real options" that can be exercised or, on the contrary, extinguished at the right moment (Courtney, Kirkland and Viguerie, 1997; McGrath, 1999). Attempts at reproducing natural selection, however, do not always produce the expected results and raises several issues.

One issue derives from the tendency of the selection process to go over-board. Contrary to the theoretical model, real selection is not "natural" but usually performed by a few overwhelmed individuals who do not always possess the required impartiality and competencies. The selection process will be as effective as these individuals who perform it. Furthermore, selection practices tend to mirror the culture of the company that puts them in place. Risk adverse companies impose exceedingly stringent criteria (e.g. Eastman Kodak's OI and NOD), bureaucratic ones set up complex and discouraging procedures (e.g. Ohio Bell's "Enter-prize Program") and mono-lithic companies encourage decision makers to seek consensus, thus slowing and restricting the funding process (e.g. Schneider Electric's "Myriad Ideas"). At the end of the funnel, not surprisingly, successful projects are few and small by company standards.

The formal selection process is sometimes reinforced by selection exer-cised by an unsupportive work environment. Corporate entrepreneurs can find themselves isolated and the absence of supportive colleagues and supe-riors can erode their initial enthusiasm. When time, resources and freedom need to be continually negotiated, it takes individuals with exceptional dis-positions to thrive and bring the internal venturing process to completion (Burgelman, 1983 ASQ).

Another issue derives from the fact that the selection process tends to eliminate both ideas *and* individuals. This can result in discouragement, and even resentment, especially in organisations that stigmatise unsuccess-ful risk-takers. More restrictive entry conditions can, in fact, contribute to increasing rather than decreasing the number of viable projects and happy corporate entrepreneurs at the end of the funnel. If projects are fewer and well aligned, they receive more support and benefit from greater synergies with the existing businesses. If the "licit" domain of exploration is nar-rowed down a bit, the probability that projects end up in spinout decreases, limiting valuable managers' attrition. Furthermore, corporate entrepreneurs that pursue projects that enhance in some fundamental way their company's strategic goals will feel more confident and willing to take risks on other fronts.

The Discipline of Venture Capitalists

In the last decade, it has become popular for large companies to fashion their separate entrepreneurial entity after Venture Capital structures. Companies such as Xerox and Lucent Technologies have modelled their New Venture Divisions after Venture Capital structures and established active partnerships with external venture capitalists (Box 8.2).

Box 8.2 When venture capital is the source of inspiration

Xerox's XTV, the entrepreneurial entity in charge of exploiting Xerox's technologies, was explicitly modelled after a venture capital organisation. It performed due diligence on the ideas that Xerox's researchers proposed and evaluated them on the basis of their potential return on investment. It would then turn selected ideas into viable activities and form independent companies whose ownership was shared among Xerox and the intrapreneurs, as well as external venture capital firms. XTV's ambition was to introduce these companies on to the stock market. In order to benefit from the impartiality and good judgement of venture capitalists, as well as their often excellent network of informants, XTV instituted a syndication policy that made the financial participation of external Venture Capital funds mandatory. Temporary executives familiar with start-up management were hired to reinforce internal teams and new ventures, CEOs were recruited externally. Xerox employees willing to join XTV had to demonstrate their commitment by relinquishing all return guarantees. The relations of XTV with Xerox were at arms' length and XTV paid for the use of corporate resources and competences.

Lucent Technologies' NVG initiators described their unit as a "halfway house" combining features of both Venture Capital structures and large technological companies. From Venture Capital organisations, it adopted the "small bets" and "few wins, many losses" philosophy, the reliance on return on investment as a key evaluation criteria and value realisation via exit. The NVG was structured and operated so as to retain flexibility and responsiveness. Decisions were made frequently and quickly. NVG's managers had foregone bonuses and corporate fringe benefits but were granted phantom stock options. Over time, the NVG learned to put great emphasis on upfront evaluation and developed sophisticated due diligence methods. External venture capital funds were involved through syndication and new venture boards often included venture capitalists.

Source: Adapted from Lerner and Hunt (1998), Chesbrough (2000) and Chesbrough and Massaro (2001).

If we are to judge from these two cases, the "discipline" of venture capitalists does ensure excellent financial results. Over a short period of time, both the XTV and the NVG have given birth to a number of profitable businesses with excellent return for the investors. A majority of these businesses have been spun out, generating attractive capital gains for the parent company. However, there are also some negative aspects. The adoption of Venture Capital norms and procedures strongly differentiates the entrepreneurial entity from the rest of the organisation and can lead to its isolation. In particular, the alignment of the Corporate Venture Capital entity's salaries and rewards with those of venture capitalists, as was the case at Lucent Technologies, can raise feelings of injustice and envy and does not encourage supportive behaviours on the part of other divisions' staff. To the extent that they generate few or no synergies with the existing businesses and use resources to fund unrelated diversification, the finality of Venture Capital inspired entrepreneurial entities can appear strategically questionable. Generating and appropriating cash by exploiting the company's technologies can look to some more like a means of personal enrichment than a legitimate corporate goal. It is only when entrepreneurial entities demonstrate their usefulness for the rest of the company that they gain widespread acceptance: XTV's relations with the rest of the organisation started to improve when one of its start-ups was reacquired by Xerox and integrated within an existing operating division, making a tangible contribution to the division's performance.

A missing design principle?

The short life expectancy of Corporate Entrepreneurship Devices

The analysis of the cases at hand shows that, after a few years, many Corporate Entrepreneurship Devices go through a critical phase from which many never recover: Corporate Entrepreneurship Devices constitute "unstable organisational forms" (Kanter et al., 1990). This phenomenon is recurrent and has been mentioned by various researchers (Fast, 1978; Kanter et al., 1991b; Block and MacMillan, 1993; Gompers and Lerner, 2000).

Why do Corporate Entrepreneurship experiments tend to remain experiments and why are those in charge incapable of turning them into lasting realities? Asking these questions is tantamount to asking why, over a period of three to five years, these key actors fail to *institutionalise* Corporate Entrepreneurship; that is, turn it into a sustainable, "non expendable" (Selznick, 1957), "taken for granted" reality (Zucker, 1983), whose value for the company does not solely depend on rational/technical factors (Selznick, 1957).

Box 8.3 Gaining legitimacy: the Raytheon NPC and the Nokia NVO cases

George Freedman, Raytheon NPC's founder, showed right from the start a great concern for organisational acceptance. During the first three years of the NPC's existence, Freedman continually fought for its recognition. He positioned the NPC as a low profile, complementary service unit that did not compete with Raytheon's R&D labs. The NPC dedicated more than 50 per cent of its resources to the development of existing divisions' ideas and to solving their punctual technical problems. Technical help was not part of the NPC's chart but it was offered because "it made political and organisational sense". The tight budget of the NPC was apparent in the modest facilities it occupied. The NPC recruited engineers with both strong technical and human abilities whose task was to maintain good relations with the rest of the organisation. NPC's employees were remunerated like any other employee and motivated mainly by intrinsic rewards and the prospect of internal and external recognition. The NPC systematically tried to find "foster parents" for internally developed projects among existing divisions' managers that, in many cases, ended up thinking they were the "true parent" of the project. Once a product idea had reached the stage of prototype, it was handed over to an operating unit, which took care of its commercialisation and assumed the financial risks.

Nokia's New Venture Organization (NVO) was set up in 1998 to triage, test and develop new ideas into activities that could be divested, turned into new business groups or reintegrated within existing business groups. Its stated mission is "to look for growth opportunities that are beyond the remit of the existing businesses but within Nokia's overall vision". According to Markus Lindqvist, NVO's director of business, "NVO does not exist for itself; it exists for Nokia... if we start to do things, we don't regard them as being our own". The NVO is positioned as a service entity fulfilling an organisational mission. The NVO is an "accelerator" that speeds up the development of ideas. At any point of time, ventures can leave the NVO and reintegrate into the mainstream. A board composed of NVO, Nokia Research Center and existing business groups' managers is in charge of evaluating the ideas referred by business divisions and deciding where they should be developed (the NVO being just one possible "home"). Before any project gets validated, it is internally tested through the informal consultation of a number of recognised experts and managers. NVO employees are remunerated like other Nokia's employees (Nokia's incentive policy favours rewards based on team performance). NVO's permanent staff is limited and project team members leave the NVO when their project is sufficiently developed.

Source: Adapted from Kanter et al. (1991a), Day et al. (2001) and Doornik and Roberts (2001).

The causes, we believe, are inherent to the mindset, role and position of Corporate Entrepreneurship experiment leaders and participants. As most innovators, corporate entrepreneurs are result-driven and care little about gaining approval and legitimacy through means that are not strictly tied to performance and outcomes. One can also assume that this orientation is reinforced by individualistic traits, such as self-reliance, that do not predispose corporate entrepreneurs to mobilise collective processes in order to reach their goals. As a result, most Corporate Entrepreneurship actors count on the *legitimacy of success* to gain support for both individual projects and the overall process. But, whereas the legitimacy of success can ensure the acceptance of a single project (as in the *Barilla* case), it cannot ensure the acceptance of complex multi-project Corporate Entrepreneurship Devices, which generate, by definition, as many failures as successes. The legitimacy of Corporate Entrepreneurship has to rest on other foundations.

Institutionalising Corporate Entrepreneurship Devices

Two success stories, the Raytheon's NPC and the Nokia's NVO cases, can help us understand how Corporate Entrepreneurship Devices can gain legitimacy within the organisation and, as a consequence, stand a better chance of surviving organisational and political hardships (Box 8.3).

There are several common points between these stories, which may help explain the sustainability and success of the two Corporate Entrepreneurship Devices:

- Both entrepreneurial entities have been positioned as complementary to the rest of the organisation and service-oriented. They do not own the products or activities they develop. Their role is to perform tasks that existing divisions would perform slowly or not at all. They are useful to the existing divisions and do not compete with them.

- The managers of both entities underplay the differences between their unit and the rest of the organisation. Even if they work differently, entrepreneurial employees do not have a different status. They maintain a low profile and their compensation is aligned with that of their colleagues.
- Both entities maintain strong links with the rest of the organisation, which they constantly involve in both operational and strategic level decisions.

In both cases, Corporate Entrepreneurship experiment leaders have demonstrated to be "institutional entrepreneurs ... capable of mounting successful challenges to existing institutional arrangements" (Fligstein, 1997) by devising subtle integration strategies. By downplaying differences and isolation, they have limited the rejection reaction of established operating entities and created a climate favourable to cooperation and success. By nurturing interdependence, they have progressively "become embedded in networks, with change in any one element resisted because of the changes it would entail for all the interrelated network elements" (Zucker, 1991). They have also enlarged the range of performance criteria by which they are to be judged to include their contribution to the success of core businesses. They have become valuable to existing divisions' managers who have a direct interest in their preservation.

Successful Corporate Entrepreneurship implementation therefore relies on four underlying principles (see Figure 8.4).

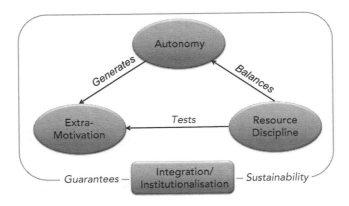

Figure 8.4 The four underlying principles of Corporate Entrepreneurship

In summary

Over the last three decades, many attempts at implementing Corporate Entrepreneurship have taken place and a great deal can be learned from them. The designers and managers of Corporate Entrepreneurship Devices start from a more solid base than their predecessors and can draw on the following findings:

☐   "Autonomy", normally restricted in large organisations, is one of the underlying principles of all successful Corporate Entrepreneurship implementation attempts. The autonomy of corporate entrepreneurs is what allows them to decide on the goals they pursue and the means they adopt. It is what allows them to freely explore the resources available in their environment and react swiftly to opportunities and threats. It is what also makes them extra-motivated, fast and responsive.

☐   Corporate entrepreneurs' autonomy is often ensured thanks to the creation of a separate entity. But organisational separation has been shown to generate problems and conflicts, which can only be avoided by establishing adequate strategic and functional links between the entrepreneurial entity and the rest of the organisation. The autonomy of entrepreneurial entities and individuals within the corporation is not a given, as in independent entrepreneurship, but a "rare resource" that has to be continually negotiated with the rest of the organisation.

☐   "Extra-motivation" is another underlying principle of Corporate Entrepreneurship implementation attempts. What motivates employees is a combination of intrinsic rewards – the appeal of developing a project from A to Z, testing oneself and being able to "make a difference" and extrinsic rewards – and company recognition under various forms, as well as, sometimes, financial incentives.

☐   However, "Extra Motivation" does not always get transformed into extra performance; corporate entrepreneurs have tacit expectations concerning what will happen during – in terms of help and support – and after the venture – in terms of rewards, recognition and reinsertion should the necessity arise. If the expectations of corporate entrepreneurs in terms of company support, rewards and recognition are not met, bad feelings can easily arise. Those who wish to encourage Corporate Entrepreneurship should ensure the sustained commitment of senior management to the experiment and its participants. Employees' expectations should be clarified and the elaboration of some form of "contract" tying the company to the corporate entrepreneur should be part of the venture approval and support process.

☐ Corporate Entrepreneurship implementation relies on a "Resource-discipline" principle, if only to balance the autonomy granted to corporate entrepreneurs. "Resource Discipline" helps reduce the risk of making costly blunders and encourages a more frugal use of resources in the process of product and business development, thus reducing the cost of innovation. Many Corporate Entrepreneurship Devices include a stage-by-stage project selection process that attempts to emulate a natural selection process. Projects are selected, vetted and moved forward in several steps, based on strict evaluation criteria. This multi-stage selection process constitutes an effective control tool for limiting the risks inherent in exploratory activities.

☐ A selection process is only as effective as the individuals who perform it. Selection practices, furthermore, tend to mirror the culture of the company that puts them in place. Risk adverse companies impose exceedingly stringent criteria, bureaucratic ones set up complex and discouraging procedures. As it constitutes the backbone of successful Corporate Entrepreneurship implementation, the design and running of a simple, fair, yet effective, selection process is a critical task.

☐ In a matter of a few years, many Corporate Entrepreneurship Devices go through a critical phase from which many never recover. To turn Corporate Entrepreneurship implementation attempts into lasting realities, those in charge have to make a deliberate effort at integrating them into the strategic and operational fabric of the company by (1) positioning entrepreneurial entities as necessary and complementary; (2) establishing strategic and operational links between entrepreneurial entities and the rest of the organisation; and (3) underplaying the differences between corporate entrepreneurs and the rest of the organisation.

To go further

Pick any two cases listed in Appendix 1. Read them and identify the main features of the Corporate Entrepreneurship Devices that are described in the case. Do these Corporate Entrepreneurship Devices share common features? Are they based on common design principles? Which ones? Compare your results to our findings and discuss them.

Conclusion 9

Whilst many companies might consider that launching a Corporate Entrepreneurship initiative is exactly what they need to find renewed innovative vigour, responsiveness, speed and ability to create wealth, it could also lead to losing their way amid paradoxes and counter-productive tensions. In order to move beyond the inherent difficulties of such initiatives and offer concrete help to businesses and corporate entrepreneurs, we would like to explore further, in this conclusion, some ideas and suggestions that will be grouped into three broad themes:

(1) Having a plan
(2) Rethinking the rules of the game to embrace Corporate Entrepreneurship
(3) Acquiring the tools to embrace Corporate Entrepreneurship

Having a plan

Pursuing Corporate Entrepreneurship should not just be giving in to the temptation to follow the latest trend. Imitating the behaviour and practices of entrepreneurs is not an obligation. For some companies, it can be vital, for others, there will be little point. The changes, pressures and turbulence that comes from the business environment are not felt in the same way and with the same intensity by all companies, which indeed occupy different competitive positions. Managers should avoid getting involved in entrepreneurial initiatives just to follow the herd or because of the positive impact it could have on the company's image. Giving in to this temptation means risking a rapid disengagement as well as compromising the credibility of practices that might one day come in very useful.

We have seen in the previous chapters that Corporate Entrepreneurship can yield different benefits – from revenue generation to innovation, from employee satisfaction to organisational learning – and that its implementation comes in different shapes and forms (from the simple entrepreneurial task force to the corporate venturing division, etc.). Pursuing Corporate Entrepreneurship requires not making a mistake in choosing the type of initiative that will be encouraged or trying to embrace everything and not hitting the right notes. It implies knowing exactly what one wants to do, why it is being done and how it will be done. That might seem obvious, but we have seen that often companies who want to get involved in Corporate Entrepreneurship have a great deal of difficulty in answering these questions.

Corporate Entrepreneurship functions on two levels, the individual and the collective, and involves three interacting elements: mindsets, behaviours and situations – all need to be analysed and taken into consideration when thinking about a Corporate Entrepreneurship initiative.

Mindsets

For individuals, one can talk about an entrepreneurial mindset and for a company one can talk about an entrepreneurial culture. How can a mindset be characterised? Through values, like a sense of risk, initiative and general attitudes such as responsibility or a willingness to change. One question to consider is, who can transmit these values and attitudes? Who can communicate a spirit or a culture of entrepreneurship? On an individual level, there is, of course, the role of the family, but also of the education system, society and other factors relating to places, professions or sectors. For a company, these values can come from a founder, managers, the organisation or the environment. They can also come from training or processes aiming to bring about cultural changes. Creating awareness through language, examples or references to internal and external models can also play an important role.

Behaviours

Behaviours can be seen, to some extent, as the concrete and tangible manifestation of mindsets. Entrepreneurial behaviours at individual and corporate levels revolve around (1) taking and accepting risks; (2) an orientation towards opportunities (identifying, selecting, seizing them and turning them into a profitable economic reality; (3) taking initiatives and responsibility;

(4) resolving management problems; and (5) working in teams and networks. One challenge relates to developing and valuing these types of behaviour in a coherent way and without provoking dissensions or exclusions. In Chapters 7 and 8, we have reviewed the main levers that can be used and organisational devices that can be put in place to do this. Another challenge is to recognise and reward the various types of behaviour that contribute, modestly or decisively, to the progress of Corporate Entrepreneurship.

Situations

Corporate Entrepreneurship initiatives are pursued in a variety of situations and for a variety of reasons: the companies involved can be large, rigid but not lacking in resources or they can be small, responsive but with limited financial and human resources. Entrepreneurship can be used to accelerate the development of one single diversification project, favour a multitude of new, innovative projects, some of which will be spun-off, or transform the way of doing business of the company as a whole. These situations are all very different (even if they share common features such as high uncertainty, risks, change, wealth creation and human/organisational dialogue) and result from the strategic choices made by the top management.

Pursuing Corporate Entrepreneurship implies having a clear strategy and choosing the elements to favour as well as the level(s) to be prioritised. Do we choose to collectively develop certain types of behaviour? Do we want to change the mindset? Or do we want to identify corporate entrepreneurs and put them in well-identified situations? From these choices, very different forms of Corporate Entrepreneurship will result. Corporate Entrepreneurship can involve a small group of selected individuals or be more widely communicated, supported by discussion and appropriate presentations. It can be driven forward by managers or be mainly the result of autonomous initiatives.

Corporate initiatives should have clear and realistic objectives and be supported by managerial levers, processes and organisational configurations that adequately translate the vision of the top management and the specificity of their situation.

Rethinking the rules of the game to embrace Corporate Entrepreneurship

The contradictions between the logic of the manager and that of the entrepreneur are often significant and can require changes to be made to the organisational framework.

Knowing the rules is taking an early stance in relation to risk, whether that means risks to be taken collectively or those authorised as part of individual initiatives. There are risks that must be accepted along with their consequences and potential failure and these principles must be integrated into managerial practices and the company culture.

Knowing the rules also enables you to choose criteria for the selection of ideas, opportunities and projects and to orient things towards certain structures or organisational forms. It is about knowing how to avoid the frustrations that can come from under-valued initiatives, if only via feedback. It is clearly defining the degree of autonomy of corporate entrepreneurs on the strategic and operational levels and specifying the principles for accessing internal and external resources. The example of companies such as 3M and Google, which have time capital to be used for individual initiatives as well as non-allocated financial capital available when needed to support new projects, constitutes a good illustration of these principles.

Finally, defining the rules of the game relates to redefining the human resources management framework. The system of sanctions and rewards can be updated, for example, in order to value creativity and taking the initiative, and not just for being good at solving problems and controlling resources efficiently. It is having a differentiated approach to people. The ideal scenario would be for everyone in the company to develop entrepreneurial behaviour. But not everyone has the same stamina, propensity for risk-taking, desire for autonomy and the need for independence and accomplishment. Not everyone has an overflowing imagination and a high level of creativity. Not everyone will join a pool of potential entrepreneurs from which will spring forth projects, processes and situations relating to entrepreneurship. The managerial and human approach must therefore distinguish at least two kinds of actors: those who want to be entrepreneurs and who have the aptitude and ability, and those who have neither the vocation nor the entrepreneurial potential, which, in a large company, would apply to a majority of individuals. But the latter should not be underappreciated or forgotten because their support and contributions are essential for the success of any initiative.

These rules should be founded on a new language integrating the key concepts of entrepreneurship and on management convictions or principles that constitute fertile supports for entrepreneurial practices. For example, one should never kill an idea, project or initiative with inappropriate words or reactions, or criticise in negative terms mistakes and failures, but encourage experience, trial and error and finally, be clear about and encourage calculated risks. The approach taken by the manager of an American company with regard to the staff gives a good example to aim for: "If you don't fail, it means you're not trying and if you don't try, you won't find new opportunities".

Acquiring the tools to embrace Corporate Entrepreneurship

Observation shows that entrepreneurs make use of techniques and tools specific to the situations in which they are involved. This section will therefore deal with some methods that can facilitate and smooth the path taken by those employees who want to embrace entrepreneurship. We will also briefly discuss how these tools might be acquired.

Contrary to what one might think, the most difficult part is not having ideas. The techniques and tools that can be used to encourage creativity are many and can, if necessary, constitute an effective support in the individual or collective processes of generating ideas. We believe that everyone can have many interesting ideas, almost on a daily basis. But from that point on, a number of problems are likely to appear. First, having an idea is not identifying an opportunity. Subsequently, if there is an opportunity, the phases of development and transformation requires a set of tools and skills, which the person who had the idea may not possess. Finally, we should point out that the process that starts with an idea and ends with something concrete that adds value to the company acts as an extremely powerful filter. One often hears that "with one hundred ideas, ten projects emerge and at the end of the process there will be one success, whether a product, service or an activity that has gotten off the ground".

In these conditions, the management techniques and tools given to corporate entrepreneurs must provide a way to evaluate opportunities, to answer the question "Am I the right person for the situation?" and to transform opportunities into projects and then into profitable economic realities.

In order to evaluate opportunities, it is necessary to know and be able to use to effective marketing tools that aim to explore the situations and environments concerned. One must know how to use research and information processing techniques and work with internal or external experts of the field and technologies concerned. Finally, one must know how to determine the needed resources as well as the economic and financial stakes.

To answer the question posed by the person/situation match scenario, one must acquire methods for individual self-diagnostics and personal development. The work consists in drawing up a corporate entrepreneur profile and checking to what extent one is suitable for the new situation, adopting a dynamic approach insofar as possible.

With the aim of transforming opportunities, a range of tools and know-how can be deployed. They relate to communication and negotiation and can be used to present, argue and convince in order to obtain a favourable decision and essential resources. They also concern recruitment and human resource assessment and management, allowing strong, complementary and motivated teams to be built.

The range of tools and know-how required is impressive and it would be unrealistic to think that a single individual can master all of them to perfection. Imperfect individual responses must give way to collective responses. It is about putting together a team whose members complement one another both technically and psychologically, alongside the sharing of values and division of roles that will allow corporate entrepreneurs to position themselves effectively in the role of leader and performer of operations.

In order to prepare those who want to experience entrepreneurial situations, a number of approaches are possible. To make them aware of the entrepreneur's ways of thinking and behaving, nothing beats contact and interaction with experienced entrepreneurs. That is why, for example, a large French company regularly sends potential corporate entrepreneurs to the United States, thus giving them the chance to talk about their projects with founders of technology start-ups in the mythical home of entrepreneurship.

Appendix 1: Our Corporate Entrepreneurship case base

First-hand cases (primary sources)

Case label	Case summary	Reference
"Developing Intrapreneurs Program" "Freco" (France)	The evolution and impact of a training programme that aimed at changing the approach to risk-taking, cooperation and innovation of "Freco"'s middle management. The programme lasted for six years and involved circa 400 managers. "Freco" is the code name of a large French utilities company. The case unfolds from 2004 to 2010.	Byrne and Fayolle (2009)
"DPF" (Divisione Prodotti Freschi) Barilla (Italy)	The story of an internal start-up set up by the owners in the late 1990s to diversify Barilla's business portfolio and restore its declining profitability. The start-up eventually became a fully fledged and highly successful new division thanks to the efforts of the highly committed and creative work team.	Bouchard (2004)
"HomeServe" (UK and France)	A description of the management and organisation of a high-growth service company that actively fosters entrepreneurial values and behaviours among its employees since its inception in 1993. The case focuses on the French subsidiary of this highly successful home repair service company. It unfolds from 1993 to 2011.	Bouchard (2012)

(Continued)

Case label	Case summary	Reference
"IDClic" *Orange* *(France)*	The story of a successful employee innovation programme that helped several thousand employees make their personal project a reality. Orange is the leading French telecom service provider. The case unfolds from 2007 to 2010.	Bouchard and Dagras (2010)
"L'Oréal" *L'Oréal* *(France)*	This case describes how under the leadership of four exceptional CEOs, the firm "L'Oréal" became the leader of the Cosmetics industry on a worldwide scale. Much of the company's success can be explained by its strong entrepreneurial orientation and culture.	Fayolle, Basso and Legrain (2008)
"MEMS Unit" "SBL" *(France)*	The story of an internal start-up created to commercialise an innovative technology and line of products and to showcase entrepreneurial spirit within SBL France. SBL is a leading oil exploration service company. The case unfolds from 2004 to 2006.	Bouchard (2009E)
"Myriad Ideas" *Schneider Electric* *(France)*	The story of an ambitious employee venturing programme put in place to foster internal growth, innovation and improve the company climate at Schneider Electric France. Schneider Electric is a leading French electrical material company. The case unfolds from 1998 to 2001.	Bouchard (2009IIC)
"TV on ADSL Project" *Orange FT* *(France)*	The story of an internal start-up created to commercialise in short order a promising new service. It eventually became a new business line of Orange FT. Orange FT is a leading French telecom service provider. The case unfolds from 2001 to 2003.	Bouchard (2009IIC)

Second-hand cases (secondary sources)

Case label	Case summary	Reference
"3M"	The portrait and history of 3M from its inception at the beginning of the century to the early 1990s with a focus on its entrepreneurially-based capability to innovate. 3M is a US based company that produces abrasives, adhesives and a host of innovative products.	Bartlett and Mohammed (1994, 1995)

(Continued)

Case label	Case summary	Reference
"Acordia"	The account of the implementation, over a ten-year period, of a highly successful entrepreneurial strategy by the CEO of Acordia, a US based insurance company. The case unfolds from 1986 to 1995.	Kuratko, Ireland and Hornsby (2001)
"Change Agent Program" *Siemens Nixdorf*	The first year of an ambitious training programme aimed at turning a selected group of middle managers into change leaders imbued with entrepreneurial values. Siemens Nixdorf is a German information systems company, part of the Siemens group. The case unfolds from 1994 to 1995.	Kanter, McGuire and Mohammed (1997)
"Corporate New Ventures (CNV)" *Procter & Gamble*	The first years of the CNV, a separate entity created to generate, develop and test new business concepts at Procter & Gamble. Procter & Gamble is a leading Consumer Goods company based in the US. The case unfolds from 1990 to 1995.	Amabile and Whitney (1997)
"Enter-Prize Program" *Ohio Bell*	The story and portrait of a successful employee innovation programme. Ohio Bell is a US based telecom service provider. The case unfolds from 1985 to 1990.	Kanter and Richardson (1991b)
"Google"	The portrait of a company that fights to maintain an "entrepreneurial" climate while increasing its revenues from $3B to $22B and the strategic and organisational challenges it faces ten years after its creation. Google is a US based company that dominates the search engine and data search industry. The case unfolds from 2004 to 2009.	Edelman and Eisenmann (2010), Groysberg, Thomas and Berkley Wagonfield (2009)
"Gore" *W.L. Gore & Associates*	The unconventional strategy, management principles and organisation of a highly innovative American company producing and commercialising advanced fibres and textiles. The case unfolds from 2000 to 2006.	Reid Townsend and Harder (2000), Hamel and Breen (2007)
"IBM Rebels" *IBM*	The story of how IBM, lagging behind every computer trend since the mainframe, caught the Internet wave in the early 1990s thanks to the talent and commitment of a group of internal "activists".	Hamel (2000)

(Continued)

Case label	Case summary	Reference
"Innovation Program Office (IPO)" *HP*	The first three years of existence of a small entity created to foster "adjacent innovation" by leveraging internal resources and competencies at HP. HP is a leading digital technology company. The case unfolds from 2006 to 2008.	Burgelman and Meza (2008)
"IE at Dow" *Dow Chemical Company (Europe)*	The case describes how a corporate entrepreneur at Dow Chemical Company shapes an internal growth venture within the company, mobilises the resources that are needed to implement the venture and achieves success. The case unfolds in Europe between 2000 and 2001.	Chakravarthy and Huber (2003)
"Joline at Polaroid" *Polaroid Corpora-tion*	The case describes how Joline Godfrey, an employee at Polaroid Corp., introduced and developed a project that could help Polaroid move to a more service- as opposed to product-oriented focus. The case, which unfolds in the late 1980s, recounts her difficulties and her eventual departure from the company.	Hill, Kamprath and Conrad (1992)
"Merlin-Gérin" *Merlin-Gérin Foundry*	The story and portrait of an entrepreneurially managed business unit within Merlin-Gérin. Merlin-Gérin is a French electrical equipment company and the case unfolds from 1959 to 1985.	Badguerahanian and Abetti (1995)
"NEES Energy Venture" *NEES*	The story and description of an entrepreneurially managed business unit within NEES. New England Electric Systems is a regional electrical network operator. The case unfolds from 1984 to 1990.	Kanter, Quinn and North (1992)
"Nespresso System (NCS)" *Nestlé*	The long and eventful story of NCS, the small affiliate of Nestlé in charge of developing the Nespresso system. Nestlé is a leading Swiss food and beverage company. The case unfolds from 1986 to 1996.	Miller and Kashani (2000)
"New Business Develop-ment (NBD) at DSM" *DSM*	A portrait of the NBD, a separate organisation created to develop promising, new business ideas within DSM. DSM is a leading Dutch chemical company. The case unfolds from 1995 to 1999.	Neiland et al. (2005)

(Continued)

Case label	Case summary	Reference
"New Product Center (NPC)" *Raytheon*	The story and evolution of the NPC, a self-standing and entrepreneurial product development centre, working both for the operating divisions of Raytheon and on its own projects. Raytheon is a military and civilian electronic equipment company based in the USA. The case unfolds from 1969 to 1985.	Kanter et al. (1991a)
"New Ventures Group (NVG)" *Lucent Technologies*	The portrait and story of an independent corporate venture organisation created to scout and commercialise promising technologies from Bell Labs. Bell Labs were part of Lucent Technologies, a leading US telecom equipment manufacturer. The case unfolds from 1995 to 2001.	Chesbrough (2000), Chesbrough and Massaro (2001)
"New Venture Organisation (NVO)" *Nokia*	The portrait of NVO, a separate organisation created to test and develop high value technologies (potential sales greater than $500M) with no "natural owners" within Nokia. The case unfolds from 1995 to 2000. Nokia, a Finnish company, was then the leader in telecom equipment and handsets.	Day et al. (2001), Doornik and Roberts (2001)
"Office of the Chief Technology Officer (OCTO)" *BP*	The accomplishments of a small autonomous "innovation team" whose mission is to accelerate the speed at which critical IT technologies are adopted by the operating divisions of BP. BP is a leading Oil and Gas company. The case unfolds from 1999 to 2005.	Wolcott and Lippitz (2007b)
"Offices of Innovation (OI) and New Opportunity Development (NOD)" *Eastman Kodak*	A detailed description of the "entrepreneurial engine" put in place by Kodak in the 1980s to "make [the company] venture operative". Our analysis focuses on the OI, created to help employees formalise and find a home for their project and the NOD, a small entity providing seed money and guidance to "orphan" projects. The case unfolds from 1983 to 1989. Kodak was then a world leading film and photography company.	Kanter et al. (1991b)

(Continued)

Case label	Case summary	Reference
"SAS"	The rapid transformation of SAS and its adoption of entrepreneurial values and behaviours under the guidance of its new CEO. SAS is the leading Scandinavian airlines company. The case unfolds from 1983 to 1985.	Kao and Blome (1986)
"Serengeti Eyewear Division" *Corning Glass*	The story and portrait of Serengeti Eyewear Division, an entrepreneurially and unconventionally managed business unit within Corning. Corning is an American glass manufacturing company. The case unfolds from 1984 to 1993.	Garvin and West (1997)
"Xerox Technology Ventures (XTV)" *Xerox*	The story of an autonomous internal venturing organisation set up to commercialise promising technologies and retain talented inventors. Xerox is a leading US based office equipment company. The case unfolds from 1990 to 1995.	Lerner and Hunt (1998)

Cases by category of Corporate Entrepreneurship

Corporate Entrepreneurship category	Corporate Entrepreneurship case
Spontaneous	IBM Rebels – IBM Joline at Polaroid – the Polaroid Corp. IE at Dow Chemical – Dow Chemical Company
Induced/Single-project	Divisione Prodotti Freschi (DPF) – Barilla Merlin-Gérin – Merlin Gérin Foundry Nespresso system (NCS) – Nestlé Serengeti Eyewear Division – Corning Glass NEES Energy Venture – NEES TV on ADSL Project – Orange FT France MEMS Unit – Schlumberger France
Induced/Multi-project	Change Agent Program – Siemens Nixdorf Corporate New Ventures division (CNV) – Procter & Gamble Developing Intrapreneurs Program – "Freco" Enter-Prize Program – Ohio Bell

(Continued)

Corporate Entrepreneurship category	Corporate Entrepreneurship case
Induced/Comprehensive	IDClic – Orange France Innovation Program Office (IPO) - HP Myriad Ideas – Schneider Electric France New Business Development (NBD) – DSM New Product Center (NPC) – Raython New Venture Organization (NVO) – Nokia New Ventures Group (NVG) – Lucent Technologies Office of the Chief Technology Officer – BP Offices of Innovation (OI) and New Opportunity Development (NOD) – Eastman Kodak Xerox Technology Ventures (XTV) – Xerox 3M Acordia Google HomeServe L'Oréal SAS (Scandinavian Airlines System) Gore (W.L. Gore & Associates)

A note on our research methodology and data sources

In order to cast a wide net on Corporate Entrepreneurship practices, we have collected and analysed the most diverse set of case studies we could possibly locate. We gathered a total of 30 cases providing detailed descriptions of Corporate Entrepreneurship in a variety of well-established firms over time. Our database contains seven first hand cases and 23 second-hand cases. The in-depth knowledge of the process and dynamics acquired through the elaboration of our seven first-hand cases was helpful in confirming theoretical assumptions and better understanding the processes at play in the second-hand cases. We were further encouraged in our decision to mix first- and second-hand case material by the arguments of several scholars (Larsson, 1993; Pawson et al., 2004; Van Aken, 2005) who urge management researchers to broaden the range of information sources. In spite of their different origins, both first-hand and second-hand cases were comparable in terms of format and richness of details, thus they were susceptible to identical treatment.

Given the heterogeneity of the phenomenon under study, working on a large number of Corporate Entrepreneurship implementation cases proved to be determining in reaching theoretical saturation. When analysing the cases in our database, we focused on various dimensions: first, the *origin* of the Corporate Entrepreneurship process – Spontaneous or Induced – the first category, which comprised three cases, being eliminated from our various studies on Corporate Entrepreneurship inducement and implementation. Second, the *scope* of Corporate Entrepreneurship implementation attempts, and third, the *constitutive elements* of Corporate Entrepreneurship implementation attempts; that is, the enablers put in place to encourage the adoption of entrepreneurial attitudes, values and behaviours. We then grouped our implementation cases according to similarities along these dimensions. Ultimately, seven very different Corporate Entrepreneurship Device models emerged. Thanks to our access to the rich data contained in the cases, we then attempted to delineate, for each Corporate Entrepreneurship Device model, an "orchestrating theme" to use Miller's (1996) terminology, covering preferred domain of application, recurrent issues and organisational implications.

First-hand cases – The seven first-hand cases included in the study were created and published over a ten-year period (2003–2012) by the authors. They provide detailed descriptions of Corporate Entrepreneurship as implemented in medium- to large-size European firms representing various industries. We personally interviewed the managers directly in charge of implementing Corporate Entrepreneurship practices and one to five other respondents per case study. We used semi-structured interviews, which lasted from one to three hours, which were conducted, for the most part, on site. Follow-up questions were submitted to the respondents by phone or email a few days later. We also reviewed and analysed companies' internal documentation (company newspapers, reports and electronic sites) when available.

Second-hand cases – The 23 second-hand cases included in our case base originate from material drawn from reputable sources such as top ranking academic journals, highly regarded professional publications or the case clearinghouses of top educational institutions. The second-hand sources were searched for in electronic databases using the following keywords: *corporate entrepreneur**, *intrapreneur** and *corporate ventur**.

When possible, multiple sources were combined and five of the Corporate Entrepreneurship cases rely on multiple sources. Sources range from academic publications or books to pedagogical cases.

Our decision to extend our sources beyond academic and peer-reviewed professional publications results from several considerations. The most important was the need to reach theoretical saturation while studying a highly heterogeneous phenomenon. Another consideration was the high quality of pedagogical cases authored by reputable scholars and published by top educational institutions. Being ourselves pedagogical cases authors and having discussed the matter with colleagues on several occasions, we believe that the data contained in published pedagogical cases, albeit selected and structured with teaching goals in mind, is no less truthful than the data contained in other types of publications, such as articles or books. Furthermore, the elements we were looking for being well grounded in theory and straightforward, the chances of missing some critical piece of information were, in our opinion, limited. We nonetheless acknowledge that, when analysing second-hand material, some constitutive element of Corporate Entrepreneurship implementation attempts might be missing, not because it is absent but because the authors failed to describe it. Here again, the large number of cases analysed was the best antidote.

References

Adler, P.S. and Kwon, D.W. (2002) Social Capital: Prospects for a New Concept. *Academy of Management Review*, 27(1): 17–40.

Amabile, T.M. and Whitney, D. (1997) *Corporate New Ventures at Procter & Gamble*. HBS No. 9-897-088. Boston, MA: Harvard Business School Publishing.

Amherdt, C.H., Dupuis-Rabasse, F., Emery, Y. and Giauque, D. (2000) *Compétences collectives dans les organisations*. Québec: Presses de l'Université de Laval.

Antoncic, B. and Hisrich, R.D. (2003) Clarifying the Intrapreneurship Concept. *Journal of Small Business and Enterprise Development*, 10(1): 7–24.

Backholm A. (1999) *Corporate Venturing: An Overview*. Helsinki: Helsinki University of Technology, Institute of Strategy and International Business. Working Paper Series1999 | 1.

Badguerahanian, L. and Abetti, P.A. (1995) The Rise and Fall of the Merlin-Gérin Foundry Business: A Case Study in French Corporate Entrepreneurship. *Journal of Business Venturing*, 10(6): 477–493.

Barry, D. (1991) Managing the Bossless Team: Lessons in Distributed Leadership. *Organizational Dynamics*, 20(1): 190–205.

Bartlett, C.A. and Mohammed, A. (1994) *3M Optical: Managing Corporate Entrepreneurship*. HBS No. 9-395-017. Boston, MA: Harvard Business School Publishing.

Bartlett, C.A. and Mohammed, A. (1995) *3M: Profile of an Innovating Company*. HBS No. 9-395-016. Boston, MA: Harvard Business School Publishing.

Bhardwaj, B.R., Sushil and Momaya, K. (2011) Drivers and Enablers of Corporate Entrepreneurship: Case of a Software Giant from India. *The Journal of Management Development*, 30(2): 187–205.

Bird, B. (1988) Implementing Entrepreneurial Ideas: The Case for Intention. *Academy of Management Review*, 13(3): 442–453.

Birkinshaw, J. (1997) Entrepreneurship in Multinational Corporations: The Characteristics of Subsidiary Initiatives. *Strategic Management Journal*, 18(3): 207–229.

Birkinshaw, J. (2003) The Paradox of Corporate Entrepreneurship. *Strategy and Business*, 30(Spring): 46–58.

Blatt, R. (2009) Tough Love: How Communal Schemas and Contracting Practices Build Relational Capital in Entrepreneurial Teams. *Academy of Management Review*, 34(3): 533–551.

Block, Z. and MacMillan, I.C. (1993) *Corporate Venturing: Creating New Businesses Within the Firm.* Boston, MA: Harvard Business School Press.

Block, Z. and Ornati, O.A. (1987) Compensating Corporate Venture Managers. *Journal of Business Venturing*, 2(1): 41–52.

Boston Consulting Group. (2014) The Most Innovative Companies 2014 Breaking through is Hard to Do, *BCG Perspectives*. www.bcgperspectives.com (Accessed 2 August 2017).

Bouchard, V. (2004) Corporate Entrepreneurship Devices: Time to Review Flawed Design Principles? *20th EGOS Conference*, Ljubljana, July 2004.

Bouchard, V. (2009E) L'intrapreneuriat, In Coster, M. (Ed.), *Entrepreneuriat* (pp. 287–312). Paris: Pearson Education.

Bouchard, V. (2009IIC) *Intrapreneuriat – Innovation et Croissance; Entreprendre dans l'Entreprise.* Paris: Dunod.

Bouchard, V. (2012) *Intrapreneurship as a Means of Achieving Growth: The Homeserve Case.* CCMP, Centrale des cas et de Médias Pédagogiques, EML-MC11L.

Bouchard, V. and Basso O. (2011) Exploring the Links between Entrepreneurial Orientation and Intrapreneurship in SMEs. *Journal of Small Business and Enterprise Development*, 18(2): 219–231.

Bouchard, V. and Bos, C. (2006) Dispositifs intrapreneuriaux et créativité organisationnelle: Une conception tronquée? *Revue Française de Gestion* 32(161): 95–109.

Bouchard, V. and Dagras, X. (2010) Tout le monde a des idées. *L'Expansion Entrepreneuriat*, 7 September 2010.

Bouchard, V. and Fayolle, A. (2013) Models of CE practice, *CE In The New Global Economic Reality Paper Development Workshop*, The Entrepreneurship Research Centre, Warwick Business School, 13–14 June 2013.

Brazeal, D., Schenkel, M. and Azriel, J. (2008) Awakening the Entrepreneurial Spirit: Exploring the Relationship Between Organizational Factors and Perceptions of Entrepreneurial Self-Efficacy and Desirability in a Corporate Setting. *New England Journal of Entrepreneurship*, 11(1): 9–25.

Brazeal, D.V. (1993) Organizing for Internally Developed Corporate Ventures. *Journal of Business Venturing*, 8(1): 75–90.

Brown, T.E., Davidsson, P. and Wiklund, J. (2001) An Operationalization of Stevenson's Conceptualization of Entrepreneurship as Opportunity Based Firm Behavior. *Strategic Management Journal*, 22(10): 953–968.

Burgelman, R.A. (1983ASQ) A Process Model of Internal Corporate Venturing in the Diversified Major Firm. *Administrative Science Quarterly*, 28(2): 223–244.

Burgelman, R.A. (1983MS) Corporate Entrepreneurship and Strategic Management: Insights from a Process Study. *Management Science*, 29(12): 1349–1364.

Burgelman, R.A. (1984) Designs for Corporate Entrepreneurship in Established Firms. *California Management Review*, 26(3): 154–166.

Burgelman, R.A. (1985) Managing the New Venture Division: Research Findings and Implications for Strategic Management. *Strategic Management Journal*, 6(1): 39–54.

Burgelman, R.A. (2005) Managing Internal Corporate Venturing Cycles. *MIT Sloan Management Review*, 46(4): 733–749.

Burgelman, R.A. and Meza, P.E. (2008) *Innovation at HP: The Role of the Innovation Program Office (IPO)*. Stanford, CA: Stanford Graduate School of Business, SM172-PDF-ENG.

Burgelman, R.A. and Sayles, L.R. (1986) *Inside Corporate Innovation: Strategy, Structure, and Management Skills*. New York, NY: Free Press.

Burgers, J.H., Jansen, J.J.P., Van den Bosch, F.A.J. and Volberda, H.W. (2009) Structural Differentiation and Corporate Venturing: The Moderating Role of Formal and Informal Integration Mechanisms. *Journal of Business Venturing*, 24(3): 206–220.

Burt, S. (1992) *Structural Holes: The Social Structure of Competition*. Cambridge, MA: Harvard University Press.

Business Dictionary. www.businessdictionary.com (Accessed 2 August 2017).

Bygrave, W.D. and Hofer, C.W. (1991) Theorizing About Entrepreneurship. *Entrepreneurship Theory and Practice*, 16(2): 13–22.

Byrne, J. and Fayolle, A. (2009) Corporate Entrepreneurship Training Evaluation: A model and A New Research Perspective. *Industry and Higher Education*, 23(3): 163–174.

Cappelli, P. (2000) A Market-Driven Approach to Retaining Talent. *Harvard Business Review*, 78(1): 103–111.

Castrogiovanni, G.J., Urbano, D. and Loras, J. (2011) Linking Corporate Entrepreneurship and Human Resource Management in SMEs. *International Journal of Manpower*, 32(1): 34–47.

Chakravarthy, B. and Huber, H. (2003) *Internal Entrepreneurship at the Dow Chemical Company*. IMD, Ref. IMD-3-1117.

Chesbrough, H.W. (2000) Designing Corporate Ventures in the Shadow of Private Venture Capital. *California Management Review*, 42(3): 31–49.

Chesbrough, H.W. and Massaro, A. (2001) *Lucent Technologies: The Future of the New Ventures Group*. HBS No. 9-601-102. Boston, MA: Harvard Business School Publishing.

Chisholm, T.A. (1987) Intrapreneurship and Bureaucracy. *S.A.M. Advanced Management Journal*, 52(3): 36–41.

Chung, L.H. and P.T. Gibbons (1997) Corporate Entrepreneurship: The Roles of Ideology and Social Capital. *Group and Organization Management*, 22(1): 10–30.

Collin, B. and Rouach, D. (2009) *Le Modèle L'Oréal – Les stratégies d'une multinationale Française*. Paris: Pearson Ed.

Copulsky, W. and McNulty, H.W. (1974) Finding and Keeping the Entrepreneur. *Management Review*, 63(4): 5–11.

Courtney, H., Kirkland, J. and Viguerie, P. (1997) Strategy Under Uncertainty. *Harvard Business Review*, 75(6): 67–79.

Covin, J.G. and Miles, M.P. (1999) Corporate Entrepreneurship and the Pursuit of Competitive Advantage. *Entrepreneurship Theory and Practice*, 23(1): 48–63.

Covin, J.G. and Slevin, D.P. (1988) The Influence of Organization Structure On the Utility of an Entrepreneurial Top Management Style. *Journal of Management Studies*, 25(3): 217–234.

Covin, J.G. and Slevin, D.P. (1989) Strategic Management of Small Firms in Hostile and Benign Environments. *Strategic Management Journal*, 10(1): 75–87.

Cyert, R.M. and March, J.G. (1963) *A Behavioral Theory of the Firm*. Englewood Cliffs, NJ: Prentice Hall.

Dalle F. (1990) L'obsession de la qualité. *Humanisme & Entreprise*, n° 183: 1–14.

Dalle, F. (2001) *L'aventure L'Oréal*. Paris: Ed. Odile Jacob.

Damanpour, F. (1991) Organizational Innovation: A Meta-Analysis of Determinants and Moderators. *Academy of Management Journal*, 34(3): 555–589.

Day, J.D., Mang, P.Y., Richter, A. and Roberts, J. (2001) The Innovative Organization: Why New Ventures Need More Than a Room of Their Own. *The McKinsey Quarterly*, 37(2): 21–31.

De Vita, R., Sciascia, S. and Alberti, F. (2008) Managing Resources for Corporate Entrepreneurship: The Case of Naturis. *International Journal of Entrepreneurship and Innovation*, 9(1): 63–68.

Dess, G.G. and Shaw, J.D. (2001) Voluntary Turnover, Social Capital and Organizational Performance. *The Academy of Management Review*, 26(3): 446–456.

Doornik, K. and Roberts, J. (2001) *Nokia Corporation Innovation and Efficiency in a High Growth Global Firm*. Case: IB-23, 2001. Stanford, CA: Stanford Graduate School of Business.

Dougherty, D. and Hardy, C. (1996) Sustained Product Innovation in Large, Mature Organizations; Overcoming Innovation-To-Organization Problems. *Academy of Management Journal*, 39(5): 1120–1153.

Edelman, B. and Eisenmann, T.R. (2010) *Google Inc*. HBS No. 9-910-036. Boston, MA: Harvard Business School Publishing.

Fast, N. (1978) *The Rise and Fall of Corporate New Venture Divisions*. Ann Arbor, MI: UMI Research Press.

Fayolle, A. (2012) *Entrepreneuriat. Apprendre à entreprendre*. 2nd edition. Paris: Dunod.

Fayolle, A., Basso, O. and Legrain, T. (2008) Corporate Culture and Values: Genesis and Sources of L'Oréal's Entrepreneurial Orientation. *Journal of Small Business and Entrepreneurship*, 21(2): 215–229.

Fligstein, N.P. (1997) Social Skills and Institutional Theory. *American Behaviorial Scientist*, 40(4): 397–405.

Floyd, S.W. and Woolridge, B. (1999) Knowledge Creation and Social Networks in Corporate Entrepreneurship: The Renewal of Organizational Capability. *Entrepreneurship Theory and Practice*, 23(3): 123–144.

Friedman, V.J. (2002) The Individual as Agent of Organizational Learning. *Californian Management Review*, 44(2): 70–89.

Frohman, A.L. (1997) Igniting Organizational Change Form Below: The Power of Personal Initiative. *Organizational Dynamics*, 25(3): 39–53.

Fry, A. (1987) The Post-It Note: An Intrapreneurial Success. *S.A.M. Advanced Management Journal*, 52(3): 4–15.

Galbraith, J. (1983) The Stages of Growth. *Journal of Business Strategy*, 3(1): 70–79.

Gartner, W.B. (1985) A Conceptual Framework for Describing the Phenomenon of New Venture Creation. *Academy of Management Review*, 10(4): 696–706.

Garvin, D.A. (2002) *A Note on Corporate Venturing and New Business Creation*. Boston, MA: Harvard Business School Publishing.

Garvin, D.A. and West, J. (1997) *Serengeti Eyewear: Entrepreneurship Within Corning, Inc*. HBS case No. 394-033. Boston, MA: Harvard Business School Publishing.

Gompers, P. and Lerner, J. (2000) The Determinants of Corporate Venture Capital Success: Organizational Structure, Incentives and Complementarities. In Morck, R.K. (Ed.), *Concentrated Corporate Ownership*. 17–50; Chicago, IL: University of Chicago Press.

Greene, P.G., Brush, C.G. and Hart, M.M. (1999) The Corporate Venture Champion: A Resource-Based Approach to Role and Process. *Entrepreneurship Theory and Practice*, 23(3): 103–122.

Groysberg, B., Thomas, D.A and Berkley Wagonfeld, A. (2009) *Keeping Google Googley*. HBS No. 9-910-036. Boston, MA: Harvard Business School Publishing.

Guth, W.D. and Ginsberg, A. (1990) Guest Editors' Introduction: Corporate Entrepreneurship. *Strategic Management Journal*, 11(1): 5–15.

Hamel, G. (2000) Waking up IBM: How a Gang of Unlikely Rebels Transformed Big Blue. *Harvard Business Review*, 78(4): 137–148.

Hamel, G. and Breen, B. (2007) *Building an Innovation Democracy in Management Innovation in Action*. Boston, MA: Harvard School Press.

Hayton, J.C. (2004) Strategic Human Capital Management in SMEs: an Empirical Study of Entrepreneurial Performance. *Human Resource Management*, 42(4): 375–391.

Hayton, J.C. (2005) Promoting Corporate Entrepreneurship through Human Resource Management Practices: A Review of Empirical Research. *Human Resource Management Review*, 15(1): 21–41.

Hayton, J.C. and Kelley, D.J. (2006) A Competency-Based Framework for Promoting Corporate Entrepreneurship. *Human Resource Management*, 45(3): 407–427.

Heller, T. (1999) Loosely Coupled Systems for Corporate Entrepreneurship: Imagining and Managing the Innovation Project / Host Organization Interface. *Entrepreneurship Theory and Practice*, 24(2): 25–31.

Herbert, T. and Brazeal, D. (2004) The Corporation of the (near) Future: Re-defining Traditional Structures for Innovation, Adaptability, and Entrepreneurship. *Journal of Business and Entrepreneurship*, 16(2): 115–140.

Hill, L.A., Kamprath, N.A and Conrad, M.B. (1992) *Joline Godfrey and the Polaroid Corporation (A)*. Boston, MA: Harvard Business School, Case 9-492-037.

Hill, S.A. and Birkinshaw, J. (2008) Strategy-organization Configurations in Corporate Venture Units: Impact On Performance and Survival. *Journal of Business Venturing*, 23(4): 423–444.

Honig, B. (2001) Learning Strategies and Resources for Entrepreneurs and Intrapreneurs. *Entrepreneurship*, 26(1): 21–35.

Hornsby, J.S., Kuratko, D.F. and Montagno, R.V. (1999) Perception of Internal Factors for Corporate Entrepreneurship: A Comparison of Canadian and U.S. Mergers. *Entrepreneurship Theory and Practice*, 24(2): 9–24.

Hornsby, J.S., Kuratko, D.F. and Zahra, S.A. (2002) Middle Managers' Perception of the Internal Environment for Corporate Entrepreneurship: Assessing a Measurement Scale. *Journal of Business Venturing*, 17(3): 253–273.

Hornsby, J.S., Naffziger, D.W., Kuratko, D.F. and Montagno, R.V. (1993) An Interactive Model of the Corporate Entrepreneurship Process. *Entrepreneurship Theory and Practice*, 17(2): 29–37.

Hughes, M., Hughes, P. and Morgan, R.E. (2007) Exploitative Learning and Entrepreneurial Orientation Alignment in Emerging Young Firms: Implications for Market and Response Performance. *British Journal of Management*, 18(4): 359–375.

Ireland, R., Covin, J. and Kuratko, D. (2009) Conceptualizing Corporate Entrepreneurship Strategy. *Entrepreneurship Theory and Practice*, 33(1): 19–46.

Kanter, R.M. (1985) Supporting Innovation and Venture Development in Established Companies. *Journal of Business Venturing*, 1(1): 47–60.

Kanter, R.M. and Richardson, L. (1991) Engines of Progress: Designing and Running Entrepreneurial Vehicles in Established Companies - The Enter-Prize Program at Ohio Bell, 1985–1990. *Journal of Business Venturing*, 6(3): 209–229.

Kanter, R.M., McGuire, J.F. and Mohammed, A. (1997) *The Change Agent Program at Siemens Nixdorf*. HBS Case, No. 9-396-203. Boston, MA: Harvard Business School Publishing.

Kanter, R.M., Quinn, G. and North, J. (1992) Engines of Progress V: NEES Energy Inc., 1984–1990. *Journal of Business Venturing*, 7(1): 73–89.

Kanter, R.M., North, J., Bernstein, A.P. and Williamson, A. (1990) Engines of Progress: Designing and Running Entrepreneurial Vehicles in Established Companies. *Journal of Business Venturing*, 5(6): 415–430.

Kanter, R.M., Richardson, L., North, J. and Morgan, E. (1991b) Engines of Progress: Designing and Running Entrepreneurial Vehicles in Established Companies; The New Venture Process at Eastman Kodak, 1983–1989. *Journal of Business Venturing*, 6(1): 63–82.

Kanter, R.M., North, J., Richardson, L., Ingols, C. and Zolner, J. (1991a) Engines of Progress: Designing and Running Entrepreneurial Vehicles in Established Companies; Raytheon's New Product Center, 1969–1989. *Journal of Business Venturing*, 6(2): 145–163.

Kao, J. and Blome, J. (1986) *Scandinavian Airlines System*. HBS Case No. 9-487-041. Boston, MA: Harvard Business School Publishing.

Katz, J. and Gartner, W.B. (1988) Properties of Emerging Organizations. *Academy of Management Review*, 13(3): 429–441.

Kuratko, D.F. and Montagno, R.V. (1989) The Intrapreneurial Spirit. *Training and Development Journal*, 23(10): 83–87.

Kuratko, D.F., Covin, J.G. and Garrett, R.P. (2009) Corporate Venturing: Insights from Actual Performance. *Business Horizons*, 52(5): 459–467.

Kuratko, D.F., Hornsby, J.S. and Goldsby, M.G. (2004) Sustaining Corporate Entrepreneurship: A Proposed Model of Perceived Implementation/Outcome Comparisons at the Organizational and Individual Levels. *International Journal of Entrepreneurship an Innovation*, 5(2): 77–89.

Kuratko, D.F., Ireland, D.R. and Hornsby, J.S. (2001) Improving Firm Performance through Entrepreneurial Actions: Acordia's Corporate Entrepreneurship Strategy. *Academy of Management Executive*, 15(4): 60–71.

Kuratko, D.F., Montagno, R.V. and Hornsby, J.S. (1990) Developing an Intrapreneurial Assessment Instrument for an Effective Corporate Entrepreneurial Environment. *Strategic Management Journal*, 11(1): 49–58.

Larsson, R. (1993) Case Survey Methodology: Quantitative Analysis of Patterns Across Case Studies. *Academy of Management Journal*, 36(6): 1515–1546.

Lerner, J. and Hunt, B. (1998) *Xerox Technology Ventures: March 1995*. HBS Case No. 9-295-127. Boston, MA: Harvard Business School Publishing.

Lerner, M., Azulay, I. and Tishler, A. (2009) The Role of Compensation Methods in Corporate Entrepreneurship. *International Studies of Management and Organization*, 39(3): 53–81.

Luchsinger, V. and Bagby, D.R. (1987). Entrepreneurship and Intrapreneurship: Behaviors, Comparisons, and Contrasts. *S.A.M. Advanced Management Journal*, 52(3): 10–13.

Lumpkin, G.T. and Dess, G.G. (1996) Clarifying the Entrepreneurial Orientation Construct and Linking it to Performance. *Academy of Management Review*, 21(3): 135–172.

Lumpkin, G.T., Cogliser, C.C. and Schneider, D.R. (2009) Understanding and Measuring Autonomy: An Entrepreneurial Orientation Perspective. *Entrepreneurship Theory and Practice*, 33(1): 47–69.

MacMillan, I.C., Block, Z. and Narasimha, P.N. (1986) Corporate Venturing: Alternatives, Obstacles Encountered, and Experience Effects. *Journal of Business Venturing*, 1(2): 177–191.

Marseille, J. (2009), *L'Oréal. 1909–2009*. Paris: Editions Perrin.

McGrath, R. (1999) Falling Forward: Real Options Reasoning and Entrepreneurial Failure. *Academy of Management Review*, 24(1): 13–30.

Merrifield, D.B. (1993) Intrapreneurial Corporate Renewal. *Journal of Business Venturing*, 8(5): 383–389.

Miles, M.P. and Covin, J.G. (2002) Exploring the Practice of Corporate Venturing: Some Common Forms and Their Organizational Implications. *Entrepreneurship Theory and Practice*, 26(3): 21–40.

Miller, D. (1983) The Correlates of Entrepreneurship in Three Types of Firms. *Management Science*, 29(7): 770–770.

Miller, D. (1996) Configurations Revisited. *Strategic Management Journal*, 17(7): 505–512.

Miller, D. and Friesen, P.H. (1982) Innovation in Conservative and Entrepreneurial Firms: Two Models of Strategic Momentum. *Strategic Management Journal*, 3(1): 1–25.

Miller, J. and Kashani, K. (2000) *Innovation and Renovation: The Nespresso Story*. Lausanne: IMD International.

Mintzberg, H. and Waters, J.A. (1982) Tracking Strategy in an Entrepreneurial Firm. *Academy of Management Journal*, 25(3): 465–499.

Monsen, E., Patzelt, H. and Saxton, T. (2010) Beyond Simple Utility: Incentive Design and Trade-offs for Corporate Employee-Entrepreneurs. *Entrepreneurship Theory and Practice*, 34(1): 105–130.

Morris, M., van Vuuren, J., Cornwall, J. and Scheepers, R. (2009) Properties of Balance: A Pendulum Effect in Corporate Entrepreneurship. *Business Horizons*, 52(5): 429–440.

Morris, M.H. and Kuratko, D.F. (2002) *Corporate Entrepreneurship*. Orlando, FL: Harcourt College Publishers.

Morris, M.H. and Jones, F.F. (1999) Entrepreneurship in Established Organizations: The Case of the Public Sector. *Entrepreneurship Theory and Practice*, 24(1): 71–91.

Morse, C.W. (1986) The Delusion of Intrapreneurship. *Long Range Planning*, 19(6): 92–95.

Mucchielli, R. (2002) *Le Travail en Equipe: Clés Pour Une Meilleure Efficacité Collective*. Paris: ESF.

Naffziger, D.W., Hornsby, J.S. and Kuratko, D.F. (1994) A Proposed Research Model of Entrepreneurial Motivation. *Entrepreneurship*, 18(3): 29–42.

Naffakhi, H. (2011) Une étude exploratoire sur le rôle des équipes entrepreneuriales dans l'émergence des compétences, *7ème Congrès de l'Académie de l'Entrepreneuriat et de l'Innovation*, Paris, 12–15 October 2011.

Neiland, R., Leuverink, I., van Hoven, F., van Wely, M. and Vanhaverbeke, W. (2005) *Stamypor*. Case 905M72. London, ON: Richard Ivey School of Business.

Pawson, R., Greenhalgh, T., Harvey, G. and Walshe, K. (2004) *Realist Synthesis: An Introduction, RMP2. ESRC Research Methods Programme*. Manchester: University of Manchester.

Pinchot, G. (1985) *Intrapreneuring: Why You Don't Have to Leave the Corporation to Become an Entrepreneur*. New York, NY: Harper and Row.

Pinchot, G. (1987) Innovation through Intrapreneuring.*Research Management*, 30(2): 14–19.

Reid Townsend, D. and Harder, J. (2000) *W.L. Gore & Associates*. Ref. UV3176, Charlottesville, VA: Darden Business Publishing, University of Virginia.

Robbins, S., Judge, T. and Gabilliet, P. (2006) *Comportements Organisationnels*. Paris: Pearson Education.

Rousseau, D.M. (1995) *Psychological Contracts in Organizations: Understanding Written and Unwritten Agreements*. Thousand Oaks, CA: Sage Publications.

Russell, R.D. (1999) Developing a process model of intrapreneurial systems: A cognitive mapping approach. *Entrepreneurship Theory and Practice*, 23(3): 65–84.

Sathe, V. (1985) Managing an Entrepreneurial Dilemma: Nurturing Entrepreneurship and Control in Large Corporations? In Hornaday, J.A. et al. (Eds) *Frontiers of Entrepreneurship Research* (pp. 636–656). Wellesley, MA: Babson College.

Schmelter, R., Mauer, R., Börsch, C. and Brettel, M. (2010) Boosting Corporate Entrepreneurship through HRM Practices: Evidence from German SMEs. *Human Resource Management*, 49(4): 715–741.

Selznick, P. (1957) *Leadership in Administration*. New York, NY: Harper and Row.

Shane, S.A. (2003) *A General Theory of Entrepreneurship: The Individual-Opportunity Nexus*. Cheltenham, UK and Northampton, MA: Edward Elgar Publishing.

Shane, S. and Venkataraman, S. (2000) The Promise of Entrepreneurship as a Field of Research. *Academy of Management Review*, 25(1): 217–226.

Sharma, P. and Chrisman, J.J. (1999) Towards a Reconciliation of the Definitional Issues in the Field of Corporate Entrepreneurship. *Entrepreneurship Theory and Practice*, 3(3): 11–28.

Shepherd, D.A. and Krueger, N.F. (2002) An Intentions-Based Model of Entrepreneurial Teams' Social Cognition. *Entrepreneurship Theory and Practice*, 27(2): 167–185.

Siegel, R., Siegel, E. and MacMillan, I.C. (1988) Corporate Venture Capitalists: Autonomy, Obstacles and Performance. *Journal of Business Venturing*, 3(3): 233–247.

Simsek, Z., Lubatkin, M., Veiga, J. and Dino, R. (2009) The Role of an Entrepreneurially Alert Information System in Promoting Corporate Entrepreneurship. *Journal of Business Research*, 62(8): 810–817.

Startup Commons. www.startupcommons.org (Accessed 2 August 2017).

Stevenson H.H. (2000) *Why Entrepreneurship Has Won*. Coleman White Paper, USASBE Plenary Address, 2000, 8 p.

Stevenson, H.H. and Gumpert, D.E. (1985) The Heart of Entrepreneurship. *Harvard Business Review*, 23(2): 85–94.

Stevenson, H.H. and Jarillo, J.C. (1990) A Paradigm of Entrepreneurship: Entrepreneurial Management. *Strategic Management Journal*, 11(5): 17–27.

Stopford, J.M. and Baden-Fuller, C.W.F. (1994) Creating Corporate Entrepreneurship. *Strategic Management Journal*, 15(7): 521–536.

Sykes, H.B. (1992) Incentive Compensation for Corporate Venture Personnel. *Journal of Business Venturing*, 7(4): 253–265.

Sykes, H.B. and Block, Z. (1989) Corporate Venturing Obstacles: Sources and Solutions. *Journal of Business Venturing*, 4(3): 159–167.

Thornberry, N. (2001) Corporate Entrepreneurship: Antidote or Oxymoron. *European Management Journal*, 19(5): 526–533.

Thornberry, N. (2003) Corporate Entrepreneurship: Teaching Managers to be Entrepreneurs. *The Journal of Management Development*, 22(4): 329–344.

Tzeng, C. (2009) A Review of Contemporary Innovation Literature: A Schumpeterian Perspective.*Innovation: Management, Policy and Practice*, 11(3): 373–394.

Van Aken, J.E. (2005) Management Research as a Design Science: Articulating the Research Products of Mode 2 Knowledge Production in Management. *British Journal of Management*, 16(1): 19–36.

Venkataraman, S., McGrath, R.G. and MacMillan, I.C. (1992) Progress in Research on Corporate Venturing. In Sexton, D.L. and Kasarda, J.D. (Eds), *The State of the Art of Entrepreneurship*. (pp. 487–517) Boston, MA: PW-Kent Publishing Company.

Vesper, K.H. (1984). Three Faces of Corporate Entrepreneurship. In Hornaday, J.A., Tarpley, Jr, F.A., Timmons, J.A. and Vesper, K.H. (Eds), *Frontiers of Entrepreneurship Research* (pp. 294–320). Wellesley, MA: Babson College.

Von Hippel, E. (1977) Successful and Failing Internal Corporate Ventures: An Empirical Analysis. *Industrial Marketing Management*, 6(3): 163–174.

West, G.P. (2007) Collective Cognition: When Entrepreneurial Teams, Not Individuals, Make Decisions. *Entrepreneurship Theory and Practice*, 31(1): 77–102.

Westfall, S.L. (1969) Stimulating Corporate Entrepreneurship in U.S. Industry. *Academy of Management Journal (pre-1986)*, 12(2): 235–246.

Wiklund, J. and Sheperd, D. (2005) Entrepreneurial Orientation and Small Business Performance: A Configurational Approach. *Journal of Business Venturing*, 20(1): 71–91.

Wolcott, R.C. and Lippitz, M.J. (2007a) The Four Models of Corporate Entrepreneurship. *MIT Sloan Management Review*, 49(1): 75–82.

Wolcott, R.C. and Lippitz, M.J. (2007b) *BP's Office of the Chief Technology Officer: Driving Open Innovation through an Advocate Team*. KEL366, Kellogg School of Management. Evanston, IL: NorthWestern University.

Zahra, S.A. (1991) Predictors and Financial Outcomes of Corporate Entrepreneurship: An Exploratory Study. *Journal of Business Venturing*, 6(4): 259–285.

Zahra, S.A. (1993) A Conceptual Model of Entrepreneurship as Firm Behavior: A Critique and Extension. *Entrepreneurship Theory and Practice*, 17(4): 5–21.

Zahra, S.A. and Covin, J.G. (1995) Contextual Influences on the Corporate Entrepreneurship–Performance Relationship: A Longitudinal Analysis. *Journal of Business Venturing*, 10(1): 43–58.

Zahra, S.A., Jennings, D.F. and Kuratko, D.F. (1999) The Antecedents and Consequences of Firm-Level Entrepreneurship: The State of the Field. *Entrepreneurship Theory and Practice*, 24(2): 45–65.

Zahra, S.A., Nielsen, A.P. and Bogner, W.C. (1999) Corporate Entrepreneurship, Knowledge and Competence Development. *Entrepreneurship Theory and Practice*, 23(3): 169–189.

Zucker, L.G. (1983) Organizations as Institutions. In Bacharach, S. (Ed.), *Research in the Sociology of Organizations, Vol. 2* (pp. 1–47). Greenwich, CT: JAI Press.

Zucker, L.G. (1991) The Role of Institutionalization in Cultural Persistence. In Powell W. and DiMaggio P. (Eds), *The New Institutionalism in Organizational Analysis* (pp. 83–107). Chicago, IL: Chicago University Press.

Index

Page numbers in *italics* indicate tables and figures; those in **bold** indicate box features.